Exploring England's Heritage

D1031336

YORKSHIRE TO HUMBERSIDE

Jane Hatcher

Published in association with

English ✛ Heritage

London: HMSO

Jane Hatcher decided to be an architectural historian during a childhood spent exploring York's historic buildings. She now lives in a quaint house in Richmond, North Yorkshire, and as well as researching, lecturing and writing, enjoys hard work in her roof-level garden, from which there are marvellous views.

The author worked as a fieldworker on the Re-Survey of Listed Buildings in North Yorkshire in 1984–8. She is actively involved in York Georgian Society, the Yorkshire Buildings Preservation Trust, Richmondshire Museum and Richmond and District Civic Society. She is a committee member, appointed by the Secretary of State for the Environment, of the Yorkshire Dales National Park; a trustee of the North East Civic Trust; and a Pageant Master of the Company of Cordwainers of the City of York.

Her other published works include *The Industrial Architecture of Yorkshire, Richmondshire Architecture* and *George Cuit the elder (1743–1818)*.

© *Jane Hatcher 1994*
Applications for reproduction should be made to HMSO
ISBN 0 11 300026 X

British Library Cataloguing in Publication Data

A CIP catalogue record for this book
is available from the British Library

HMSO publications are available from:

HMSO Publications Centre
(Mail, fax and telephone orders only)
PO Box 276, London SW8 5DT
Telephone orders 071-873 9090
General enquiries 071-873 0011
(queuing system in operation for both numbers)
Fax orders 071-873 8200

HMSO Bookshops
49 High Holborn, London WC1V 6HB
(counter service only)
071-873 0011   Fax 071-873 8200
258 Broad Street, Birmingham B1 2HE
021-643 3740   Fax 021-643 6510
33 Wine Street, Bristol BS1 2BQ
0272 264306   Fax 0272 294515
9–21 Princess Street, Manchester M60 8AS
061-834 7201   Fax 061-833 0634
16 Arthur Street, Belfast BT1 4GD
0232 238451   Fax 0232 235401
71 Lothian Road, Edinburgh EH3 9AZ
031-228 4181   Fax 031-229 2734

HMSO's Accredited Agents
(see Yellow Pages)

and through good booksellers

Printed in the UK for HMSO
Dd 294228 C80 3/94

Contents

Foreword

Today as midsummer approaches, Oxford is crammed with tourists. The roads near
my office are choked with open-topped buses, their multilingual commentaries
extolling the virtues of the city, while the pavements are impassable with crocodiles
of visitors, eyes glued on the coloured umbrellas of determined guides. Dons wearing
full academic dress attempt to make their way to and from the Examination Schools,
to the delight of foreign photographers, and might as well be extras employed by the
Tourist Board.

Oxford, Stratford-on-Avon and London together make up the golden triangle –
golden, that is, to the tour operators – and millions of tourists are led through their
crowded streets each year. The great majority of those who visit Oxford come for
only a few hours, then move on to Stratford to stay overnight before returning to
familiar London. It is London that takes the brunt. Westminster Abbey will be host
to over 3 million, more than 2 million will visit the Tower of London, and then of
course there are the museums and art galleries welcoming their annual tidal wave.
Tourism, as governments are pleased to remind us, is one of Britain's biggest
industries.

Looking at the tired, bewildered faces of the tourists off-loaded and scooped up
again outside Oxford's St Giles, I long to grab them and say, 'It's all right – this is *not*
what it's about. England is a beautiful, gentle country full of fascinating corners,
breathtaking sights – an eclectic mix of unsurpassable quality. All you need is
someone with vision to show you how to start looking.'

Well, people with vision, as well as the knowledge of our cultural heritage and the
ability to communicate, are not in ample supply, but the members of the team
assembled to write the eleven volumes of *Exploring England's Heritage* share these
qualities in abundance. Each author has a detailed and expert involvement, not only
with the region they are writing about, but also with the buildings, the earthworks,
the streets and the landscapes they have chosen to introduce us to. These guides are
no mere compilations of well-worn facts, but original accounts coloured by the
enthusiasm of people who know what makes a particular site so special.

Each volume introduces more than 100 places. Some are well known (who would
dare to omit Stonehenge or Hadrian's Wall?); others are small-scale and obscure but
no less interesting for that. We are led down alley-ways to admire hidden gems of
architecture, into churchyards to search for inscribed stones and along canals to
wonder at the skills of our early engineers. And of course there are the castles, the
great houses and their gardens and the churches and cathedrals that give England its
very particular character.

Exploring England's Heritage does not swamp you in facts. What each author
does is to say, 'Let me show you something you might not have seen and tell you why
I find it so particularly interesting.' What more could the discerning traveller want?

Barry Cunliffe

Acknowledgements

Many friends and acquaintances have given help and encouragement, but particular mention must be made, in alphabetical order, of Keith Chapman, Brenda Heywood, the late Herman Ramm, Shirley Thubron, Robert White, Mark Whyman and Margaret Wills who have all most generously shared their expertise.

I am indebted to John Hutchinson for allowing me to use some of his beautiful water-colour paintings, which were photographed by Bob Skindle of the York office of the Royal Commission on the Historical Monuments of England (RCHME), who has also specially taken some of the other illustrations. Staff of the National Monuments Record at RCHME, particularly Ian Leith, gave considerable help in locating photographs, as did Lucy Bunning of the English Heritage Photograph Library. Author and publisher are grateful to the following, in addition to those mentioned above, for permission to reproduce their photographs and drawings: John Bethell; Bradford Public Libraries; British Waterways; Cleveland County Libraries; Anthony Wells Cole and Christine Stokes of Temple Newsam House; Olive Cook for Edwin Smith's photographs; *Country Life*; the *Darlington and Stockton Times*; Harrogate Resort Services; Donald Innes Studios; Helen M Kirk of York Georgian Society; Kirkleatham Museum; Landmark Trust; W Lynch; Malton Museum; Mansell Collection; National Trust; Norfolk Museums Service (Norwich Castle Museum); North Yorkshire County Council; the *Northern Echo*; Rotherham Central Library; Christopher Stell; Peter H Townsend; Wakefield Metropolitan District Council; L P Wenham; B J A Wragg; York Archaeological Trust; and Yorkshire Dales National Park. Maps and plans have been drawn by the English Heritage Illustrators' Office.

HMSO's keen editor Ruth Bowden has provided a lot of support and her colleague Stuart McLaren has tracked down illustrations from many sources.

I am most grateful to Brian Anthony for asking me to provide one of the volumes in this regional series. I greatly enjoyed revisiting old haunts, and even discovering a few new treasures.

Notes for the Reader

Each site entry in *Exploring England's Heritage* is numbered and may be located easily on the end-map, but it is recommended especially for the more remote sites, that the visitor makes use of the relevant Ordnance Survey map in the Landranger series. The location details of the site entries include a six-figure National Grid reference, e.g., NZ 174006. Ordnance Survey maps show the National Grid and the following 1:50,000 maps will be found useful: 88, 91, 92, 93, 94, 98, 99, 100, 101, 104, 105, 106, 107, 111, 112, 113.

The Humber estuary can only be crossed by the Humber Bridge, which joins Hessle on the north side with Barton-upon-Humber on the south side. Readers are advised to bear this in mind when planning visits to the various Humberside sites in the book.

Readers should be aware that while the great majority of properties and sites referred to in this handbook are normally open to the public regularly, others are open only on a limited basis. A few are not open at all, and may only be viewed from the public thoroughfare. In these circumstances readers are reminded to respect the owners' privacy. The *access codes* in the heading to each gazetteer entry are designed to indicate the level of public accessibility, and are explained below.

Access Codes

[A] site open for at least part of the year
[B] site open by appointment only
[C] site open by virtue of its use, e.g., a road or bridge
[D] site not open but which may be seen from the public highway

Abbreviations

BJAW	BJA Wragg	JH	Jane Hatcher
C	Cleveland	LPW	L P Wenham
CCL	Cleveland County Libraries	LT	Landmark Trust
CL	*Country Life*	NT	National Trust
CS	Christopher Stell	NY	North Yorkshire
DIS	Donald Innes Studios	NYCC	North Yorkshire County Council
EH	English Heritage	RCHME	Royal Commission on the Historical
ES	Edwin Smith		Monuments of England
H	Humberside	SY	South Yorkshire
HMK	Helen M Kirk	WY	West Yorkshire
JB	John Bethell	YAT	York Archaeological Trust

The county names and boundaries used in this guide were correct at time of going to press, and are those used prior to the Local Government Commission review of 1993.

Further Information

Further details on English Heritage, the Landmark Trust and the National Trust may be obtained from the following addresses:

English Heritage (Membership Dept), PO Box 1BB, London W1A 1BB

Landmark Trust, 21 Dean's Yard, Westminster, London SW1P 3PA

National Trust (Membership Dept), PO Box 39, Bromley, Kent BR1 1NH

Introduction

The three counties of North, West and South Yorkshire, together with Cleveland and Humberside, constitute a region richly diverse in landscape, geology, historical development and architecture. The landscape varies from the flat lands around the Humber and Tees estuaries, and the plains of York and Mowbray, to the rolling chalk hills of the Yorkshire Wolds, and the steeper hills and dales of South, West and North Yorkshire. It is characterised by great contrasts between industrial conurbations and wild moorland spaces. The settlements now regarded as Teesside are only a short distance from Cleveland's small villages, and many of West Yorkshire's industrial towns are surprisingly close to the Yorkshire Dales. The region also contains a long stretch of coastline, used first for trade, much later for pleasure.

Buildings reflect geology in their materials. There are sandstones of various qualities, poorer ones used as rubble, better ones as fine ashlar, and some strata used for roofing slates. Magnesian limestone is a noticeable regional characteristic. Many lowland areas had a tradition of timber-framed construction, superseded, as supplies of stout timber were exhausted, by bricks and tiles baked from local clays. Humberside, one of the first areas in the country to use brick, was closely followed by York, where plain tiles were made long before other areas developed pantiles.

There are historic towns and cities, and settlements much more recent in origin, some in places barely inhabited before. The converse is evident also: Swaledale, one of the region's remotest areas, had a considerable prehistoric population. The Yorkshire Wolds, also with relatively few present-day inhabitants, were home to early peoples with complex cultures. There is extensive evidence of Roman occupation, and current archaeology is adding considerably to knowledge of the so-called Dark Ages, after the end of Roman influence and before the Norman Conquest.

The Normans have bequeathed us several fine castles, the history of which chart waxing and waning fortunes of leading families of their day. The relative proximity to the troubled Scottish border prompted many other families to construct fortified houses, an important regional category justifying its own chapter in this book. Some settlements were defended by fortifications, and these are included in the chapter on castles.

From the Anglo-Saxon period onward, but particularly in the medieval period, during times both troubled and calm, fine churches were built throughout the region. Good examples of Anglo-Saxon, Norman and medieval churches survive in such numbers that the process of selection for this volume has been extremely difficult. There are also many of post-Reformation date. Many, in addition to intrinsic beauty and historical interest, contain monuments which provide links with the people responsible for other great structures.

The region covered by this volume is quite exceptionally rich in the remains of medieval monastic houses, which constitute the most unique aspect of its heritage. The region's wild, open spaces were ostensibly the attraction, but every attempt was made to cultivate and civilise those extensive tracts which were in monastic ownership.

More peaceful post-medieval times saw large and comfortable houses built, particularly in the country, but also in towns and cities, and many of the nationally known architects worked in the region. The grander houses expressed the wealth and political aspirations of their builders, and many were given elaborately landscaped gardens.

The region also has an outstandingly important industrial heritage (covered in chapters 7 and 8). More aware than

The River Swale above Keld. ES

(*Left*) Whitby, North Yorkshire. ES

(*Right*) Easby Abbey, the refectory. EH

many of this, as author of *The Industrial Architecture of Yorkshire* (1985), I hope a fair balance of the heritage overall has been achieved. I have similarly tried to resist the temptation of giving undue prominence to the heritage covered in my volume on *Richmondshire Architecture* (1990).

The selection of a limited number of sites, determined by constraints of space, has been particularly difficult, all the more so as an overwhelming choice is presented by the region's considerable wealth of heritage. The author has for these reasons been obliged regretfully to exclude some sites which the reader may have enjoyed while others have been excluded as access is limited or impossible. The introductions to each chapter therefore direct the reader to some sites which are omitted from the gazetteer but which are well worth a visit or provide interesting points of comparison.

I greatly enjoy lecturing on and guiding people around the many places in the region which are particularly precious to me. This volume is an attempt to share with readers, whether residents or visitors, just a few of those places which make my home country so unique.

Antiquities: Prehistoric–Medieval

Yorkshire, Humberside and Cleveland have seen many types of occupation. Prior to the Roman period, Yorkshire and Cleveland were part of the larger territory of the Brigantes, while North Humberside was that of the Parisi, and South Humberside part of the lands of the Coritani. The Roman conquest provided over three centuries of more standardised culture (AD 71–410), and the typical Roman plan, a rectangle with rounded corners reminiscent of a playing card, was applied to most structures from small signal stations to huge fortresses.

Incursions and native unrest, as well as changes of mind among those in authority, resulted in a succession of phases of reconstruction. These are usually described in relation to the emperor of the day, such as Agricolan or Trajanic, and late repairs are often Theodosian. The post-Roman period saw a wide variety of occupation, sophisticated and primitive, so confusing that the blanket term 'Dark Ages' is used to describe several centuries.

What structures there are of this period, such as the post-Roman tower inserted into the Roman defences near **York**'s Multangular Tower (13, NY) are subject to widely differing interpretation by scholars. Most evidence occurs at ecclesiastical sites and many churches, such as **Stanwick** (10, NY), contain carved stones, both Christian and non-Christian. Easby (17, NY) near Richmond has an exceptionally fine early cross, and St Hilda's Church, Hartlepool (37, C), the tombstone of the 7th-century nun Hildithryth.

Archaeological excavation in the region has produced important evidence of prehistoric occupation of great diversity, such as the rare Mesolithic lakeside settlement at Star Carr, Seamer near Scarborough (NY), but not necessarily in a form or location suitable for public access – a main requirement for inclusion in this series. However,

attempts have been made to present some of the sites to the public, one such being Staple Howe at Knapton near Malton (NY), where the positions of excavated hut circles of the late Bronze–early Iron Age have been marked with concrete posts.

Standing stones provide more tangible evidence of early activity, and those included here are of national importance: the **Rudston Monolith** (9, H) is Britain's tallest standing stone, and the **Devil's Arrows** (5, NY) form an impressive if mysterious monument. Of similar late-Neolithic–early Bronze Age date are the Thornborough Circles near West Tanfield (NY), three henges and an earlier cursus, but they are not all easy to see. The cursus near Scorton (NY) is also inaccessible.

A major archaeological study in the Yorkshire Dales National Park, where prehistoric field systems and enclosures probably survive better than anywhere else in the country, has discovered an enormous number of important early sites, and a project in Swaledale has been investigating overlying field systems going back to the Neolithic period. Like so many such remains, they are best seen from the air during light snow cover.

Maiden Castle (6, NY) in Swaledale is an important monument in its own right, but is also almost like a hillfort, a category by definition often relatively inaccessible, as is the important Iron Age hillfort at Ingleborough (NY). Roads pass around the hillfort at Almondbury (WY) near Huddersfield, but later modifications confuse inexpert interpretation of the site. Easier to understand are the great and famous earthwork fortifications at Stanwick, (10, NY) which clearly defended an Iron Age site of particular wealth and status.

Straddling the cultural boundary between native and Roman settlements is the sophisticated regional capital Isurium Brigantum at **Aldborough** (1, NY) near Boroughbridge. York (13,

One of the standing stones of the Devil's Arrows. ES

A re-erected column from the basilican hall of the *principia* of York Roman fortress.
LPW

villas known in the area, such as that excavated at Beadlam (NY), none is accessible to the public, although some tessellated pavements are displayed in museums (see 9, H). Several great houses contain classical statuary, notably Castle Howard (66, NY) and Newby Hall (74, NY).

Linear earthworks are particularly difficult to assign to a date unless they have been excavated, and sometimes even when they have. In some cases leading scholars differ completely in their interpretation, as at **Danes Dyke** (4, H) near Flamborough, which has been ascribed to both the Iron Age and the so-called Dark Ages, but is here interpreted as the latter. Another example is Scots Dike, which forms the eastern boundary of Richmond (90, NY).

Excavations at York have uncovered, as well as Roman material, extensive remains of the timber structures of Viking Jorvik and, less famously, details of medieval industry, including a horner's workshop. At the time of writing, excavations are unearthing an Anglian settlement at West Heslerton near Malton (NY), and also invaluable evidence of a farm and its associated fields at a medieval moated site at Wood Hall near Selby (NY).

Wharram Percy (11, NY), one of the country's best preserved, and researched, deserted medieval villages, has also produced evidence of occupation back to Neolithic times, and so encompasses almost the whole spectrum of this chapter.

1

Aldborough Roman Town, N Yorkshire
AD 2nd–4th century

SE 405667. Aldborough, just SE of Boroughbridge, 12 miles (19.3 km) N of Wetherby via A1(T)

[A] EH

Isurium Brigantum was the *civitas* capital of the Brigantes, the largest tribe of Roman Britain. The settlement was a high-ranking civilian, not military, administrative centre. Its plan,

NY) retains substantial remains of the great legionary fortress of Eboracum; at **Malton** (7, NY), quite a lot can be seen of the Roman fort, and much is known about its *vicus*. **Bainbridge** (2, NY) in Wensleydale, when viewed from a distance gives an impression of an entire upland fort, and a rarer phenomenon, a Roman training camp, is well presented at **Cawthorn** (3, NY) near Pickering.

An amazing stretch of Roman road can be seen on **Wheeldale Moor** (12, NY) near Whitby, and another section is exposed high up in the Pennines on Blackstone Edge (WY), between Yorkshire and Lancashire. A Roman bridge abutment survives at **Piercebridge** (8, NY), and part of a Roman signal station at Scarborough Castle (53, NY). Another signal station is mentioned under Saltburn (92, C). It is regrettable that of the many fine Roman

enclosing some 54 acres (22 ha) was, however, conventional, and the streets formed a rectilinear grid pattern. Its longer axis was orientated north–south, and the present village occupies rather more than the southern half.

The exposed Roman remains, from the south-west corner of the town, include several lengths of town wall, built in red sandstone on a chamfered plinth, with a corner tower and parts of two interval towers. Between, the width of lost sections of the wall is picked out by edging in the grass.

A short field walk leads to two small summer-house-like structures, each protecting a tessellated pavement, found in the early 19th century and preserved *in situ*. Both are from the same large town house. The first pavement has a central panel in which an animal, perhaps a lion, sits under a stylised tree. Around it concentric bands of geometric patterns include two types of plaited guilloche motif, the colours red, black and white. The second, in red, black,

white and yellow, has a central panel with an eight-pointed star, surrounded by plaiting and deep Greek key design. Outside the second building are pieces of Roman stonework.

The high quality of the museum's contents reflects the status of this Roman settlement. The bronze jewellery and other items of personal dress and adornment are particularly fine, and there are good bone objects, and interesting pieces of iron horse-harness. Complete pots include some of imported Samian ware, also examples made in Britain, both locally and particularly in the Nene valley. Larger stone items include two Roman milestones, and several querns.

The tall shaft of a late-medieval cross stands in the village on the line of the road linking Isurium Brigantum's west and east gates. At the intersection of the Roman town's two main roads, probably on the site of its *forum*, is the Church of St Andrew. A Roman sculpture of the god Mercury inside its west end suggests

there was a nearby temple to that deity. The north aisle has at the east end a large 14th-century brass to William de Aldeburgh. On the north chancel wall, above the clergy vestry medieval door, is a monument to Andrew Wilkinson, 18th-century Member of Parliament for Aldborough, which was a 'Rotten Borough'. South of the church in the churchyard a ledger tombstone, perhaps of 14th-century date, is rather unusually carved with the upper torso of a woman, with arms folded, in bas-relief.

2

Bainbridge Roman Fort, N Yorkshire
AD 1st–4th century

SD 937901. On hillside 274 yds (250 m) E of Bainbridge (on A684 Hawes–Aysgarth road)

[D]

There is no public access to this site, so it is only described briefly, but the fort's distinctive and characteristic outline can be clearly seen from the north side of Wensleydale. One of the best-investigated Roman upland forts, it typifies the incredibly large number of alterations undertaken by the Roman army after the initial Agricolan construction in timber, through the rebuilding in stone, and culminating in a Theodosian late restoration, although there is no evidence of preceding enemy destruction. Even, or perhaps especially, at this remote location there was a *vicus*, or civilian settlement, which was given defences, probably in the early 3rd century.

The Roman name was Virosidum, very appropriately meaning 'high seat', for it guarded a pass through the Pennines. The line of the Roman road survives as a track leading south-west from Bainbridge, up over Cam Fell, past Ingleborough and on to Lancaster. To the south lay the fort at Ilkley (WY), to the east the legionary fortress at York (13, NY), and to the north the even wilder Stainmore Pass and its forts in Cumbria.

Aldborough Roman town, tessellated pavement. EH

Bainbridge Roman fort from the air. YAT

approaches the south gate, skirts the south-west corner, crosses ditches and rampart to enter the fort by the west gate, passes the central site of the *principia* building, and leaves by the east gate.

Immediately to east the walk skirts the north rampart of the strangely coffin-shaped practice camp, where Roman soldiers learned fort construction techniques. This provides extremely rare and important evidence of the thorough campaigning training that professional Roman soldiers had when establishing their frontier on Hadrian's Wall. A thoughtfully placed seat provides an enjoyable view northwards. Ahead is the impressively tall rampart, single ditch and west gate of the larger third camp, temporarily occupied by the soldiers while working on their other constructions here. The return journey passes more of the practice camp's rampart. Further east, the fourth camp, probably also temporary, lies outside the currently accessible area.

3

Cawthorn Roman Camps, N Yorkshire
AD 1st–2nd century

SE 783894. 4 miles (6.4 km) N of Pickering, N of A170 Helmsley–Pickering road. From N end of Cropton village, 1½ miles (2.4 km) E towards Newton-on-Rawcliffe. Car park ¼ mile (0.4 km) up track from road; some of the access paths to the monument are surfaced suitably for wheelchairs

[A] North York Moors National Park

Of the four camps, arranged in a west–east line, the western two are accessible. The first of these, a typical Roman fort, rectangular with rounded corners and central gateways in its sides, is surrounded by double ditches flanking a still-impressive turf rampart. The path

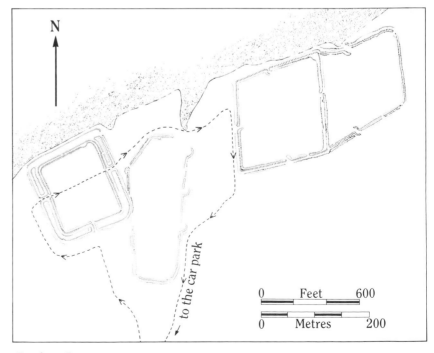

Cawthorn Roman camps. EH

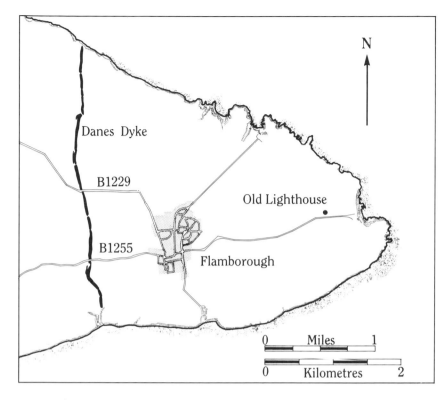

Danes Dyke. EH

4

Danes Dyke, Flamborough, Humberside
Probably AD 5th–6th century

TA 213697. Crossed by B1255 and B1229 roads ¾ mile (1.2 km) W of Flamborough and 2 miles (3.2 km) NE of Bridlington

[A]

The Yorkshire Wolds have many boundary ditches of Iron Age date, but this massive linear earthwork is different. It is of an amazing scale, with huge banks, over 18 ft (5.4 m) high in places, flanking a 60 ft (18.2 m) wide, steep ditch which is partly rock-cut, and anyone falling into it would, even now, have some difficulty climbing out. The average height of the bank top above the ditch bottom is 26 ft (8 m), and the combined width of ditch plus bank is 44 yds (40 m). There were two openings through the defence. Although its date is open to debate, the probability is that this is an earthwork of the Dark Ages.

It runs almost due north–south, right across the whole of the Flamborough peninsula, a length of 2¼ miles (3.6 km). Clearly a fortification, it faces west, and thus defends the 5 square miles (13 sq km) of land to its east, which had probably been colonised by a foreign landing force who wished to claim and fortify the beach head. Danes Dyke is seen to best effect where it is crossed by the B1229 Bempton–Flamborough road, but it can also be enjoyed 1 mile (1.6 km) further south, where there is a well-signposted car park, picnic area and nature trail immediately south of the B1255 Bridlington–Flamborough road. This area has an attractive Victorian garden setting, although it includes a dene which can be confused with Danes Dyke.

5

Devil's Arrows, Boroughbridge, N Yorkshire
Late Neolithic–early Bronze Age

SE 391665. Alongside road from Boroughbridge to Roecliffe, just E of A1

[D]

These primeval megaliths are within deafening earshot of the thunderingly noisy modern A1 as it bypasses the old bottleneck of Boroughbridge, and passengers being driven south along the A1 enjoy the best, if dynamic, vantage point for two of them. There are three, in a row, but spaced as for four with one missing. Early antiquarians recorded more standing stones from this monument – the ceremonial purpose of which is still unclear – and it has been suggested that there were twenty-three in all. The area has a series of circular earthwork henges, the best examples being a contemporary group of three, 328 yds (300 m) in diameter, with 10 ft (3 m) high banks and ditches, plus cursus, at Thornborough near West Tanfield (NY, SE 286795).

The nearest source for the Devil's Arrows' millstone grit is over 6 miles

Devil's Arrows, two of the megaliths. ES

(9.6 km) away in the Knaresborough area. Hewn as vast horizontally shaped blocks, they have been set up on end, at right angles to their original strata. Weathering over the last few millennia has given their surfaces vertical striation. Each monolith is squarish in plan, tapering upwards to the top. Their heights above ground vary between 18 ft (5.4 m) and 22 ft (6.7 m). One stands in a tree-sheltered enclosure at the edge of the Boroughbridge–Roecliffe road, the other two in an arable field immediately to its north.

6

Maiden Castle, N Yorkshire
Early Iron Age

SE 021981. Opposite Healaugh, S of minor road through Harkerside on S side of Swaledale

[D]

Mid-Swaledale is rich in earthworks, many of them connected with early methods of farming, particularly on the north bank of the River Swale. Here on Harkerside there are several linear earthworks, as well as the enclosure known as Maiden Castle, which is reminiscent of an Iron Age hillfort, although it is on the side, not the top, of a hill. The hillside on which it lies is heather-covered, but this is such a major earthwork that it stands out, shaped, it has been observed, like a comice pear.

The area enclosed is almost 1 acre (0.4 ha), and was levelled to provide a better base for the hut circles which have been traced within it. The settlement is enclosed by a ditch, which appears remarkably deep as it is set between two banks, originally walled. The field system associated with the enclosure suggests a date in the mid– late 1st millennium BC.

On the east side of the enclosure there is an avenue, about 164 yds (150 m) long, still impressively flanked by the fallen remains of its walls. This feature may have been added, perhaps to form a drove road for the later Iron Age pastoral farmers.

7

Malton Roman Fort and *Vicus*, N Yorkshire
AD 1st–4th century

SE 791717. Orchard Fields, alongside A169 Pickering road ¼ mile (0.4 km) N of Malton town centre

[A]

Derventio fort, which lies parallel to the road, is aligned geographically diagonally, so its corners face the four cardinal points. By turning left after entering the site, visitors can follow the fort's north-west ditch and rampart, skirt its north corner, marked by a tablet, and follow its north-east side down past the east gate. The east corner of the rampart, over 10 ft (3 m) high, is particularly impressive. A further defensive bank continues from this corner to protect the *vicus*, or civilian settlement, which lay between the fort

Malton, part of the building dedication stone erected by the Ala Picentiana.
MALTON MUSEUM

and the River Derwent.

The Roman history of Malton is complex: the fort had many phases. The surviving earthworks are substantially Trajanic, from soon after AD 100. Derventio was an important fort, strategically placed half-way between the fortress at York (13, NY) and the east coast. It was also unusually large. A building dedication inscription found in 1970 provided the explanation: it housed a cavalry regiment of the Roman auxiliary army, the Ala Picentiana, and such a unit required accommodation for horses as well as men.

Major excavations in 1949–52 and 1968–70 provided detailed knowledge of the *vicus*. It too had a chequered history. In its heyday in the early 4th century it contained large and comfortable Roman houses, stone-built with lozenge-shaped roof slates, the interiors with painted wall plaster and central heating below mosaic pavements. The writer, in slimmer youthful days, spent one memorable afternoon in 1969 in a hypocaust, excavating its stoke-hole: the crouched position was rewarded by retrieval of five well-nigh complete pots. They were of various designs, and of the grey ware produced at Crambeck, just a short distance down the River Derwent.

Malton Museum displays many finds. Pottery has included, as well as the ubiquitous Samian, Crambeck ware painted with faces, also unusual sherds of grey ware, made nearby at Norton, decorated with smith's tools, perhaps votive offerings to the god Vulcan. Glass fragments encompass high-quality vessels, fine beads and bracelets, and even window glass. Among bone artefacts are four braiding tablets for weaving.

The *vicus* has also produced important evidence of Iron Age occupation. Several bone items represent weaving, notably a complete toggle, still with its end pegs, and combs. Two chalk figurines, both male as they wear swords, are particularly attractive. They are of a type associated with East Yorkshire, the land of the Parisi, a tribe of peaceful herdsmen who practised elaborate burial rites, carefully interring dismantled carts with their dead.

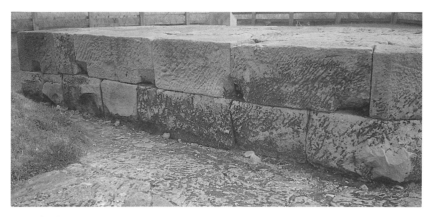

Piercebridge Roman bridge abutment, showing slots for diagonal timbers supporting the carriageway. JH

8

Piercebridge Roman Bridge Abutment, N Yorkshire
AD 2nd–4th century

NZ 214154. ½ mile (0.8 km) SE of Piercebridge, on S bank of River Tees and on E side of B6275 Piercebridge–Scotch Corner road

[A] EH

The George, the nearby ancient coaching inn, is here because for centuries this has been an important river crossing. The present, partly early 16th-century bridge, names the village of Piercebridge across in County Durham, occupying the site of the Roman fort which guarded the Tees crossing of Dere Street, the major route linking northern Britain to York.

Sometime in the mid-2nd century, the original Roman bridge was washed away by flooding. The Tees was then already moving its course northwards and the Roman engineers decided to rebuild it on a new site about 220 yds (200 m) downstream from the old one, necessitating the realignment of Dere Street. The Tees has continued to move north, silting up its Yorkshire bank, and leaving some distance from the river the south end of the Roman bridge, which was discovered in 1972 during gravel workings. The first information board is placed at what was the centre of the river in Roman times.

In view of the river's turbulent nature, the Romans first constructed a paved surface, which had two purposes. It provided a level foundation for the bridge piers and, perhaps more importantly, smoothed the river flow under the bridge. Where the water was most powerful, in the middle of the river bed, the large blocks forming the pavement are fastened together with iron cramps, set in lead.

Each of the nine evenly spaced piers was five-sided, in plan a squarish rectangle with pointed upstream end to break the force of water. The piers have been damaged by subsequent floods, but much of the south bank abutment remains *in situ*, of similar plan, but with longer pointed profile. The two surviving courses are of huge blocks of stone, very accurately squared so as to fit tightly together, with draughted margins to the tooling. Some of the horizontal joints are again cramped, and on the same principle the courses were held together vertically by dowels. The quality of the abutment stonework is a great credit to the Roman masons' work.

The Yorkshire side of the river was clearly already silting up even as the bridge was being constructed, for the design was changed while work was still in progress. It was decided to extend out a causeway, supported by a revetment wall, to carry the road further out towards the river. The first two piers were dismantled, but the abutment was left in position. The causeway revetment is of conspicuously less substantial stonework.

The bridge carriageway was carried on a wooden superstructure with oblique bracing timbers. Five angled slots for these are visible on the abutment. Two are incomplete, indicating the change of plan, but they do show that the bridge was 6¾ yds (6.1 m) wide – wide enough for two-way traffic.

9

Rudston Monolith, Humberside
Late Neolithic–early Bronze Age

TA 097678. Rudston, on B1253 Sledmere–Bridlington road. In churchyard

[D]

Perched somewhat incongruously outside the north-east corner of the church, which it dwarfs, this monument to pre-Christian ceremonials is the tallest standing stone in Britain, 24¾ ft (7.5 m) high and 6 ft (1.8 m) wide. It has been roughly dressed into a rectangular section, and presents a rather gaunt profile, its pointed top now capped in lead to protect it from the weather. The megalith is of grey gritstone, and is thought to have been dragged the 10 miles (16 km) from the nearest outcrop at Cayton Bay.

The Church of All Saints seems relatively young by comparison, despite a Romanesque tower and Early English arcades, and its Decorated chancel has a piscina and three-seat sedilia with crocketed gables. Good Victorian fittings include a bejewelled stone reredos with Minton tiles, and stalls for a numerous choir. Beside the Romanesque drum-shaped font, with geometric decoration of alternating octagons and circles, is a grave cover of *c.*1300, the raised cross with stepped base and indented arms. This light church with little, but mainly good 19th-century stained glass, also has a modern window by Harry Harvey of York showing The Sower.

The area was important in Roman as

Rudston, the monolith beside the east end of the church. BJAW

10
Stanwick Fortifications, N Yorkshire
AD 1st century

NZ 179112. Forcett, on B6274
Barnard Castle–Richmond road. On
E edge of village beside road to
Aldbrough St John

[A] EH

The area with public access (labelled
'Guardianship Site' on plan) is a tiny
part of the great earthworks which
enclose over 690 acres (280 ha) of land
in the Stanwick–Forcett area. Other
lengths of rampart are clearly visible
from public roads and footpaths.
Stanwick was famously excavated by Sir
Mortimer Wheeler in 1951–2, and the
area in the guardianship of English
Heritage is that which he considered to
be of outstanding significance.

The fortifications were constructed
by the Brigantes, the largest tribe of Iron
Age England, only a few years before the
Romans annexed their territory.
Brigantia occupied most of northern
Britain, stretching from the east coasts
of Northumberland, Durham and
Cleveland, across to the west coasts of
Cumbria and Lancashire, and down as
far as Derbyshire.

Brigantia was ruled by a queen,
Cartismandua, who was sympathetic to
the Romans, and encouraged extensive
trading with them. Her consort,
Venutius, however, was anti-Roman, as
were many Brigantes. Inevitably, their
domestic squabbles developed into
internecine warfare and Cartismandua
both sought and received help from the
Romans. Thus when, in AD 71, the
Roman Emperor Vespasian ordered
Petillius Cerialis, his newly appointed
Governor of Britain, to conquer
Brigantia, it seems likely that
Cartismandua negotiated a treaty with
the Romans while Venutius held out.

Wheeler suggested that Stanwick
may have been his headquarters, an
assembly area for his section of the tribe.
There is, however, clear evidence from
more recent excavations that both
Roman pottery and building materials
were in use within the fortifications

well as prehistoric times. In the Hull and
East Riding Museum at Hull are some
very fine tessellated pavements from a
4th-century Roman villa near Rudston.
One has a central panel showing a
helmeted charioteer returning in victory
from a race, facing us from behind his
four frisky horses, carrying a palm in his
left hand and the victory wreath in his
right. Corner panels show the four
seasons as female heads. Another mosaic
shows a rather grotesque nude Venus,
juggling with an apple and a mirror,
being wooed by a Triton carrying
Cupid's upright torch. This pavement
too has panels showing the four seasons,
this time as animals – bull, lion, leopard
and stag. A third pavement, from a bath
suite, shows aquatic creatures, notably
rather engaging dolphins.

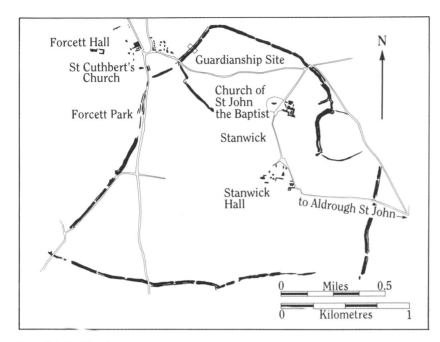

Stanwick fortifications. EH

from about AD 40, so there must have been earlier co-operation. The Brigantes, or at least one of their royal households, had a luxurious life-style, particularly in terms of high quality metalwork, both of iron and bronze.

The English Heritage site lies on the edge of Forcett village, beside the road leading east towards Aldbrough St John, which passes through an opening in the rampart. The section of rampart that is open to the public stands to such a considerable height that steep steps have necessarily been provided to climb up onto it, but from the top there is a fine view of the earthworks to the west towards Forcett Church.

The access path continues for a short distance along the top of the rampart, with the deep ditch outside the fortifications to the left: a grassed area of rampart clearly shows its rounded inner profile. A path descends into the excavated section of ditch, steps having been formed down into the flat bottom, cut into the bedrock at a depth considerably below natural ground level. From this point there is a good view back up to the reconstructed stone wall revetting the vertical outer face of the rampart.

The redundant Church of St John the Baptist in the hamlet of Stanwick contains many medieval effigies and tombstones, also several fine monuments to the Smithson family. Carved stones of earlier date include the shaft of a 9th-century cross outside the church. The churchyard's curvilinear shape may imply that it is of pre-Conquest date.

11

Wharram Percy Deserted Medieval Village, N Yorkshire

SE 859645. 6 miles (9.6 km) SE of Malton, off B1248. Signposted from Wharram le Street. Car park on Thixendale road; walk down to site takes about 10 mins, between wild-flower-covered banks

[A] EH

The study of deserted medieval villages was pioneered here, as forty-one seasons of excavation (1950–90) were devoted to establishing the community's 5,000-year history. Successively overlying one

another are the habitations and agricultural systems of Neolithic, Bronze Age, Iron Age, Romano-British, Anglo-Saxon, Norman and medieval periods. The site, a chalk plateau of the Yorkshire Wolds 492 ft (150 m) above sea level, was chosen for its seven springs.

The population peaked c.1300, when the Percy family were manorial lords, hence the name. The village was deserted when early-Tudor grazing of sheep for wool production, needing only a few shepherds, became more profitable than the labour-intensive growing of crops in strips on open fields. Arable farming resumed late in the 18th century, after the 'Agricultural Revolution' introduced new crops enabling more meat-producing animals to be over-wintered. The only roofed structure now on the site was built as cottages within a late 18th-century farm courtyard complex.

An ancient hollow-way, probably of prehistoric origin, formed the main street of the medieval village, which consisted of tofts – houses with rear yards, behind which were crofts – enclosed paddocks. Toft boundaries generally remained constant, although houses within them were rebuilt over the centuries. Most early medieval peasant houses here were gable-end to the street. Several later medieval dwellings were long-houses, with a room for humans at one end, another for animals at the downhill end, and a cross-passage between. The manor houses were of more complex plan, and built of more substantial materials. The millpond-cum-fishpond at the south end of the village has been restored as a nature reserve.

The Church of St Martin remained in use to serve other villages, but reflected the inhabitants' waxing and waning fortunes. The Anglo-Saxon settlement's small chapel was replaced by an early 12th-century church of nave and apsidal-ended chancel. A west tower was soon added, then a south aisle which necessitated the insertion of an arcade in the south nave wall. A 13th-century north aisle required a north arcade, and the chancel was slightly enlarged by squaring off its east end. The last

Wharram Percy, interior of the blocked south arcade. BJAW

Wheeldale Moor Roman road. JH

expansion was a 14th-century north chancel chapel; by c.1500 the aisles, surplus to requirements, were demolished and the arcades blocked, and in the early 17th century the chancel shrank.

The ruined church combines above-ground archaeology and architectural history. A forlorn half of the small embraced tower survived collapse during a thunderstorm in 1959: a Perpendicular stage over its 12th-century tower arch and belfry window had required the building of a buttress to the south nave wall, re-using medieval grave covers. The south aisle windows, including two late 14th-century straight-headed two-light replacements, were recycled into the double-chamfered south arcade, its east round arch with chevron decoration. Pointed-arched Decorated windows are reset in the pointed-arched north arcade. Excavation of more than 700 burials – dating from a period of over a millennium – in the church and environs has produced evidence of population health across all strata of society, from manorial lords and priests to the humblest peasants.

12

Wheeldale Moor Roman Road, N Yorkshire
AD 1st–4th century

SE 805975. 9 miles (14.5 km) N of Pickering as the crow flies. S of A171 Guisborough–Whitby road, through Egton and Egton Bridge, and 5 miles (8 km) from Key Green over the moors to the site

[A] EH

Here, a mile-long stretch of Roman road is exposed to the elements. Part of what was known for centuries as Wade's Causeway, it presents an impressive picture, crossing a spectacular area of heather-covered moorland. The road is of even width, cambered in textbook fashion to throw off the wet, culverted over small streams. The road structure is exposed: the smooth top surface is missing. It connected the Roman fort at Malton (7, NY) with the coast, somewhere near Whitby, although its continuation beyond Grosmont has not been traced.

Originally it was a trade route, particularly for jet, found near Whitby and much prized by the Romans for jewellery and ornaments. In the second half of the 4th century, as a defence against invasion in the aftermath of barbarian attacks, the Romans constructed a series of signal stations on the east coast (53, NY). Roads linked the signal stations at Saltburn and Goldsborough with Malton and, ultimately, the great military fortress at York (13, NY), and this road probably formed part of that network.

13

York Roman Fortress and *Colonia*, N Yorkshire
AD 1st–5th century

SE 602521. York city centre

In Britannia the Romans had three permanent regional military command headquarters, that for northern Britain being at York – Eboracum – which also became a *colonia*, one of the four

York, the Multangular Tower, with neat Roman stonework below irregular medieval masonry. YAT

highest-ranking civilian towns in the province, and the only place in Britain to be both. Two Roman emperors died in York while visiting the province, Septimius Severus in AD 211, and Constantius Chlorus in AD 306. The army marched north from Lincoln to York in AD 71. York was first garrisoned by the Ninth Legion, then by the Sixth. A legion consisted of 5,000–6,000 men, all professional soldiers, arranged in 80-strong centuries, grouped in cohorts.

The great military fortress of Eboracum was sited on the north-east bank of the River Ouse, where all the visible Roman remains are to be found. A bridge linked it to the *colonia*, across the river, occupied by civilians, many of whom are known by name from their tombstones. Some of these, with many other finds of outstanding importance,

are housed in the Yorkshire Museum in the Museum Gardens, York.

The fortress, in plan a larger version of a Roman fort, was initially surrounded by clay-and-turf ramparts with a wooden pallisade, defended on the outside by a ditch. At each corner was a tower, regularly spaced along each side were interval towers, and a gateway in each side led to the grid pattern of streets. The defences were rebuilt in stone in the 2nd century, partly renewed in the 3rd, the river front again in the early 4th century.

Near the medieval Monk Bar, and visible from the city walls just to its south, is the uncovered 3rd-century fortress east corner tower, built by the Sixth Legion's Tenth Cohort. The rectangular tower is set behind the rounded corner of the fortress wall,

standing here to its parapet walk height. The hump inside the tower is the earlier rampart, into which the tower was cut. The fortress wall is exposed as far as the next interval tower.

The fortress west corner, the Multangular Tower, stands above ground in the Museum Gardens, with an adjoining stretch of wall to the first interval tower. Constantius Chlorus rebuilt the river frontage on a grand scale, with eye-catching bands of red tile decoration. The towers here are polygonal, project from the fortress wall, and rose above the wall parapet. The neat, regular stonework of the legionary builders contrasts with the Multangular Tower's larger and less regular upper masonry, added when it was increased in height to form part of the city's medieval defences.

A gate to its north gives access to the interior, where the red tile band is seen more clearly. A path to the north-east, between the Roman wall exterior and medieval wall interior, leads to a small tower of cruder workmanship dating from the Dark Ages, after the Roman army withdrew from Britain. Beyond it are sections of York's defensive ramparts from Roman to medieval times.

The two main streets of the fortress, Via Praetoria (now Stonegate) and Via Principalis (now Petergate), met in the centre outside the *principia* or legionary headquarters. This lies below York Minster (44, NY), and is partly visible in its 'Foundations' display. On the north-east side of the *principia*, which was built around a quadrangle, was a basilican hall of similar proportions to the Minster nave. One column from the basilica has been re-erected opposite the Minster south door: it seems somewhat crude in finish, but would have been coated in plaster, painted to look like marble. Part of an internal fortress bath-house can be viewed inside The Roman Bath public house in St Sampson's Square.

2

Monastic Houses

This chapter reflects the large number and high quality of monastic sites in the region, particularly in North Yorkshire. There were two waves of conversion to Christianity, in the 7th and 11th centuries. No buildings from the former period survive in the area, largely due to destruction by 9th-century Danish invasions, but the later Whitby Abbey (94, NY) occupies the clifftop site of its 7th-century predecessor, one of the most hallowed early Christian shrines of Northumbria. This earlier origin may be the reason why its location is so different from the valley-bottom sites of most other religious houses here described.

Some monasteries owed their foundation to late 11th-century zeal when, in the aftermath of the Norman Conquest, there was a Benedictine revival. St Mary's Abbey in York (in the Museum Gardens in the city centre) was endowed with its site by William Rufus, who himself laid the foundation stone in 1088. The surviving main fragment, the north aisle nave wall, is from a Geometric-period rebuilding, but the adjoining Yorkshire Museum contains much of the chapter house, plus the statues of apostles and prophets, carved to a particularly high sculptural quality, which adorned its walls.

Most of the region's monasteries were established in the 12th century, when the Cistercian, Augustinian and Premonstratensian orders were more popular. The Cluniac order was represented for a time at **Monk Bretton** (22, SY). At Old Malton (NY) a house of the Gilbertines, England's only native religious order, survives fragmentarily in the parish church.

There was inevitably much rebuilding after the original establishment, but Romanesque and Transitional architecture are well represented, particularly at Cistercian houses, where the extra accommodation needed to house the lay brothers was rarely updated. The inclusion here of six Cistercian sites (**Bewerley**, 14, NY;

Byland, 16, NY; **Fountains**, 18, NY; **Jervaulx**, 20, NY; **Rievaulx**, 25, NY; and **Roche**, 26, SY) reflects the grandeur of their ruined buildings: a seventh, Kirkstall Abbey (WY, on the A65 3 miles (4.8 km) W of Leeds city centre), where there are extensive remains, would have been included if it did not present such a depressing sight, municipal and unloved, the public excluded from all of its ruins except the cloister, because of misuse. The Augustinians have four entries also, but their houses are generally somewhat less complete.

Some foundations can claim a genealogy of almost Old Testament proportions, for Whitby begat **Lastingham** (27, NY), which is one of the few places with 11th-century architecture of monastic grandeur, followed by St Mary's Abbey at York (NY), which in turn spawned Fountains. The houses of nuns were generally poorer than those of their male counterparts, and only one nunnery earns an entry, that at **Nun Monkton** (24, NY). Of the later orders, the area boasts the country's most complete Carthusian house at **Mount Grace** (23, NY), also an unusually fine relic of the Grey Friars at Richmond (90, NY). The difference in status between abbeys and priories seems not necessarily to have been reflected in architectural quality.

The sites of religious houses offer different survivals, and the overall picture of a typical convent can only be built up in composite fashion. Sometimes the church is largely complete, as at Fountains and Rievaulx, and in other cases it has almost entirely vanished, as at **Easby** (17, NY) where, however, remains a complete late 13th-century gatehouse. The area offers an interesting range of gatehouses. Those at Monk Bretton and Bridlington are unusually wide, and Bridlington's Bayle Gate, crenellated in 1388, stands next to the Priory Church, which was once the nave of one of the wealthiest Augustinian houses. The gatehouse at

Fountains Abbey, east end in 1856.
MANSELL COLLECTION

17

Rievaulx Abbey, south choir arcade. BJAW

Kirkham (21, NY) is richly sculpted. The 14th-century gatehouse at **Thornton Abbey** (28, H) is unbelievably complex, and its architecture makes an interesting comparison with the secular Marmion Tower (58, NY).

St Mary's Abbey at York retains most of its 13th-century precinct wall, built after disputes with the citizens of York, and crenellated early in the 14th century. The grange chapel at Bewerley is a rare survival, although there is another, in secular use, at Thrintoft near Northallerton (NY). Fine medieval grave covers survive at many monastic sites.

Most of the religious houses have splendid riverside sites. Some, such as Fountains and Roche, offer a fascinating array of water courses, others, like Mount Grace, have ingeniously planned drains, or drains of monumental construction, as at Kirkham. At both Easby and Monk Bretton the reredorter drains were flushed by the mill race. Other sites provide more cerebral pleasures, such as the wonderful floor tiles at Byland or the heraldry on the gatehouse at Kirkham.

The later medieval period saw a variety of building activities. At Whitby the church was improved despite the debts of the house. At Fountains the addition of a tall tower expresses Marmaduke Huby's valiant attempt to reverse the general decline in both monastic standards and numbers. The ruins at Easby and Jervaulx, on the other hand, show clear evidence of space in the domestic buildings, which had become surplus due to declining numbers, being divided up into apartments to accommodate corrodians, who had entered into a legal contract with a religious order to receive board and lodging in return for endowment.

Northern England was generally loth to relinquish its religious houses, as is demonstrated by the passionate support here for the Pilgrimage of Grace rebellion against Henry VIII's Dissolution. As a result of this uprising, the unfortunate Adam Sedburgh, abbot of Jervaulx was hanged; the abbot of Easby actually returned and reoccupied the abbey for some months after the Dissolution.

Not all monastic sites were left as

Bewerley Grange Chapel, inscription above east window. RCHME

plundered ruins after the Dissolution. Conversion into parish churches has preserved at least part of some monastic churches, as at **Bolton** (15, NY), Bridlington and Nun Monkton. At many sites, such as Newburgh Priory, near Coxwold (82, NY), the domestic buildings were converted into secular houses. At York, the grand residence of the abbot of St Mary's ironically became the seat of the Council of the North, set up as a result of the Pilgrimage of Grace.

14

Bewerley Grange Chapel, N Yorkshire
16th century

SE 158647. Bewerley. In Nidderdale, ⅓ mile (0.5 km) S of B6265 Grassington–Ripon road, ½ mile (0.8 km) SW of Pateley Bridge

[A]

This grange of Fountains Abbey (18, NY) was one of very few to have a chapel building. It is unclear why it did so, for Cistercian lay brothers usually returned to their monastery from the granges for important services. The present chapel can be dated to *c*.1525, but that may have been a remodelling of a chapel at Bewerley before the property was granted to Fountains.

Over the east window is inscribed *soli deo honor et gloria*, and three external walls bear the initials *M H* of

Marmaduke Huby, Abbot of Fountains 1494–1526, and builder of the tower there. After the Dissolution and the Reformation, it seems likely that Bewerley Grange chapel continued in use for the celebration of Roman Catholic Mass, as did similar chapels in other areas where there were recusant families, such as the Yorkes in Nidderdale.

In 1678 Mary Yorke gave it for use as a school, and a fireplace was inserted at the west end. Entry is by an 18th-century porch, which blocked an earlier window. The chapel's mullioned windows have Tudor-arched lights, sunken spandrels and separate hood-moulds. The 17th-century cottage at the west end, added for the schoolmaster, has four-light mullioned windows under continuous hood-moulds, and ovolo kneelers. Since 1960 the building has reverted to being a chapel, open for private prayer, used for monthly services, and much cherished.

15

Bolton Priory, N Yorkshire
12th–14th and 16th century

SE 073542. Bolton Abbey, on A59 Skipton–Harrogate road. Priory on E side of B6160, just N of village

[A]

Visitors see free of charge the priory, built in a lovely multi-coloured sandstone, and its setting is gloriously

Bolton Priory, choir from the south. ES

and St Cuthbert. Mostly of c.1240, the six south windows, closely spaced and set high to avoid cloister and cellarium (which precluded a south aisle), have two lancet-like lights with transom, plate-tracery quatrefoil, small dog-tooth hood-mould, and wall-walk. Their Victorian stained glass by John C Crace, in strong blues and reds, was designed in grisaille-style by Pugin.

The roof is of 16th-century date. The east wall, its late 19th-century panel tracery painted with lilies and other flora, occupies the triple-chamfered round arch of the canons' crossing tower. The north arcade, clerestory, and north aisle west wall are all 13th century, but the north windows were enlarged in the 14th century, and their curvilinear tracery retains some medieval glass. In the north aisle are a Romanesque piscina and a medieval altar slab with five dedication crosses. The octofoil font has four traceried cusps and a shafted base.

Outside the north door is a pretty Decorated image niche. The 13th-century west front, with shafted doorway, richly moulded with delicate dog-tooth, set within and below blind arcading with vesica effect, and three tall lancets, is masked by the west tower. Begun in 1520 during the time of John Moone, the last Prior, but unfinished at the Dissolution, it rises from a tracery-panelled plinth. Deep buttresses, the offsets with animals and gablets, flank a continuously-moulded doorway within more tracery panelling. The large Perpendicular window has both plain and cinque-cusped tracery, its crocketed ogee label rising up into the sky.

In 1983 the formerly open shell was roofed to form a narthex-like porch with glazed screen. It is a successful solution, worthy of the building's distinguished previous restorations. Work in 1728 was supervised by no less a figure than Richard Boyle, 3rd Earl of Burlington, whose daughter married the 4th Duke of Devonshire, hence the estate's present ownership. The 1877 restoration was by G E Street. Fragments of domestic buildings to the south include a very large now-freestanding chimney, and to the west Bolton Hall incorporates the 14th-century gatehouse.

beautiful, so it is well worth paying dearly to use the estate car park (there is nowhere else, and it keeps the chocolate-box village uncluttered). The churchyard rates high in the league of picturesque burial plots.

Augustinian canons came in 1151. Of c.1170 is the south door and intersecting wall arcading of their ruined choir. This was lengthened c.1340, with a very large east window, and one window retains tightly curled Decorated tracery. The heightened walls have deep external buttresses, so it was also vaulted. A south chantry chapel was added, also a Decorated tomb niche. The transepts had east aisles, and two reticulated north clerestory windows survive.

At the Dissolution the laity's nave became the parish church of St Mary

16

Byland Abbey, N Yorkshire
12th–13th century

SE 549789. Byland Abbey, 2 miles
(3.2 km) S of A170 Thirsk–Helmsley
road, 1½ miles (2.4 km) NE of
Coxwold

[A] EH

The Cistercians settled here in 1177
after an incredible number of false starts
elsewhere and the ruins, Transitional in
style and in beautiful cream ashlar
sandstone, are glorious. The road cuts
through the monastic compound, and
behind the appropriately adjacent
hostelry is the gatehouse. The feature
seen first is the west front of the nave, a
distinctive profile of the huge half-
circumference of its 8½ yds (7.8 m)
diameter rose window and one flanking
turret, above three lancets linked by
narrower blind ones. The trefoiled nave
doorway surrounded by plain walling
indicates the pre-Early English period.
Doors beyond shallow stepped buttresses
clearly express the aisled plan, that to
the south round and plainer than the
north, it being logical to build the
cloister side first. Here is more evidence
than usual of the narthex.

The complete north aisle wall has
large round-arched windows in regular
bays marked externally by triple pilaster
buttresses. These resisted the aisle
vaulting, which sprang from the capitals
of shafting rising from sill-band corbels.
The nave piers were heavy and square.
Chapels were walled off from the aisle
east ends, one to the south giving the
first glimpse of the medieval floor tiles
for which Byland is famed.

The transepts were aisled, with
octofoil arcade piers: the north transept
retains shafted responds with water-leaf
capitals. The south transept east chapels
retain much original flooring, the tiles
making elaborate geometric patterns.
The tiling rose in steps towards the
altars, which partly survive, and one
chapel has its piscina, formerly with
twin canopies, the base slab having three
basins, and dog-tooth on the front edge.
Another piscina base nearby has two
basins. The four east piers of the

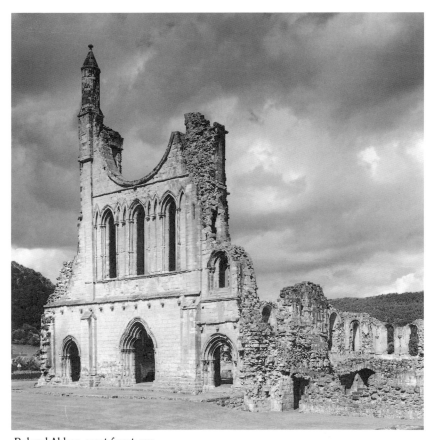

Byland Abbey, west front. EH

surprisingly short choir were keeled,
and the internal angles had corner
shafts. A section survives of the choir
stall trefoiled arcade.

Some Lombard frieze remains on the
exterior south transept east wall. A tall
fragment of its south wall demonstrates
the design of arcade, triforium and
clerestory, with pointed-arched blind
arcading at clerestory level.

Semicircular steps sweep gracefully
from nave south aisle to cloister. The
cloister arcade wall is substantially
complete, giving the profile of its ogee-
section sill. In the chapter house two
bench ends stop the stone seating, and
one rather squat pier stands, its
weathered capital of almost stiff-leaf
design. There are also some grave slabs.
Better ones can be seen in the museum,
including coped examples, also the base
of the chapter house lectern, and some
fine capitals.

17

Easby Abbey, N Yorkshire
12th–15th century

NZ 185003. Easby, 1 mile (1.6 km)
SE of Richmond, S of B6271
Richmond–Catterick Bridge road

[A] EH

The site was granted to Premonstratensian canons in 1155, but only one
pre-Gothic *ex situ* doorway survives. The
south transept east windows indicate a
c.1300 rebuilding, and soon afterwards
the north nave chapel was added,
followed by a lengthening of the aisleless
presbytery. Tomb recesses in the north
wall of the latter were probably for the
Scrope family, the abbey's generous
benefactors.

More evidence survives of the church
fittings than its fabric, including a

Easby Abbey, north chapel. JB

parclose screen with Scrope genealogy now in Wensley church (NY), and choir stalls made for Robert Bampton, the last abbot, in Richmond parish church (90, NY). Little remains of the nave except stone flooring, incised with circles on which the canons lined up before processions, and including many ornate grave covers. North of the church was the infirmary, and the abbot's first-floor suite still has a medieval chimney.

Stone benches line the rectangular chapter house, east of the cloister, into which a large east window was inserted in the 15th century, when the adjoining range was altered to provide apartments for corrodians. Over an undercroft south of the cloister was the spacious and gracious refectory, remodelled early in the 14th century, its large windows filled with Geometric tracery.

The canons' dorter was west of the cloister, above the prior's and guest suites, the latter's south window having intersecting arches. On the river side of this range, with access from all three levels and suitably offset in plan, is the reredorter. Even more ingenious was using the tail-race of the abbey's corn water-mill, north of the site, to flush the drain.

The late 13th-century gatehouse survives intact barring roof, the outer and inner single round arches set within pointed ones with stopped labels, the internal cross wall with pedestrian and vehicle arches. Quadripartite rib-vaulting over the carriageway is supported by external pilaster buttresses. First-floor two-light windows have bar tracery, and there are smaller windows in the steep gables.

The Church of St Agatha, already in existence when the abbey was formed around it, is particularly important for its rare wall-paintings, depicting scenes from the Creation and Fall of Man on the north side of the chancel, and the Nativity and Resurrection on the south wall. Of mid-13th-century date, and hardly retouched, probably drawn by one of the white canons, they give a great insight into everyday medieval life and religious belief. On the rear walls of the sedilia are contemporary portraits of three clerics.

Also in the chancel is a plaster cast of the *c*.800 Easby Cross, a sophisticated piece of sculpture giving a three-dimensional effect on the two-dimensional surfaces of its shaft. The face shows Christ in Majesty, and round arches frame the heads of the Apostles, who have shared the same Byzantine hairdresser. Birds and beasts perch in foliage scrolls on the back, and the sides

have fine interlace decoration. There are two Early English piscinas, a west wall bench, and an early 12th-century font with anthemion motif above arcading with alternate spiral columns. A pointed barrel vault supports the porch upper chamber, its access above understairs aumbries.

18

Fountains Abbey, N Yorkshire
12th–16th century

SE 274682. Studley Royal, 1 mile (1.6 km) S of B6265 Ripon–Pateley Bridge road, 3 miles (4.8 km) SW of Ripon

[A] NT

In 1132 thirteen Benedictine monks sought to reform their life at St Mary's Abbey, York. York's Archbishop Thurstan showed some sympathy and, perhaps to test their zeal, gave the dissidents land in Skelldale, 'a place remote from all the world, uninhabited, set with thorns . . . fit more, it seemed, for the dens of wild beasts than for the uses of mankind'. Doubtless aided by the fact that their number included five St Mary's office-holders and was supported by St Bernard of Clairvaux, the challenge met with worthy response, for Fountains became England's richest Cistercian abbey. It was incorporated into Studley Royal (see nos 39 and 78, NY) in 1768, and is now the most complete Cistercian abbey in the country.

This once isolated abbey has, ironically, been designated as a World Heritage site, swelling tourist numbers. Controversy originally greeted the proposal for a new Visitor Centre, but it is in this site's superlative tradition and provides a new north access, to augment that from Studley Royal to the east and the old west entrance. The author preferred the latter, for the sluice, beside the car park exit, which once controlled the corn-mill's water supply. Used long after the abbey's dissolution, this unusually well-preserved medieval water-mill, albeit without machinery, can be glimpsed from afar, the head-race full of colourful wild flowers in summer.

Near the west entrance is Fountains Hall, designed by Robert Smythson for Stephen Proctor, new landowner and aggressive Protestant, knighted by James I for fighting recusancy. Built c.1600 mainly of the softly coloured sandstone the monks quarried from the hillside to the north, it has elaborate ceilings and fine carved fireplaces.

To the west of the abbey, a small museum has a helpful abbey model and various artefacts, including an Annunciation sculpture with a lily vase almost as large as Mary and Gabriel.

West of the church was an open narthex, its delicate arcade on twin shafts with cushion capitals. In 1494 Abbot John Darnton inserted into the nave west wall a huge Perpendicular window, dwarfing the six-ordered rounded doorway below. The lay brothers' nave, large in size and robust in scale, has in each bay a round-arched clerestory window, but no triforium. The slightly pointed arcades rest on massive piers, round but with embryonic shafts to the aisles, linked with an unusual vaulting system. Best seen on the south side, each aisle bay had, at right angles to the nave axis, a round barrel vault, buttressing the clerestory walls, although the nave was unvaulted.

At the crossing are contrasts, the 12th-century south transept south chapel and, through a wide and high north transept arch, the lofty tower built c.1500 by Abbot Marmaduke Huby, a leader among English Cistercian abbots who inspired a late religious revival at Fountains. Inscriptions form string courses; stepped corner buttresses have crocketed gablets and unfilled image niches.

The Early English east arm, an early 13th-century rebuilding, was vaulted. Lancet windows in nook shafts lit the presbytery's trefoiled-canopied wall bench. The numbers of monk-priests celebrating daily Mass is reflected in the nine altars of the east transept, which developed structural problems when Abbot Darnton replaced three lancets with a vast Perpendicular east window. The flanking walls moved, and gaps at the top of some lancets were plugged by inserting carved stones – one shows an

Fountains Abbey from the east. NT

angel bearing a scroll dated *1492* on the inside, and a 'green man' on the outside.

A pleasing triple arcade on the east side of the large cloister opens into the chapter house, a fourth arch to a passage leading to the infirmary, safely detached further east. A prominent complete chimney on the south range marks the warming house, its two enormous fireplaces having flat-arched lintels with joggled voussoirs. Next west is the gracious Early English refectory, still with part of its pulpit in the west wall. Steam escaped through high-level vents from the adjacent lofty kitchen.

Domestic accommodation was duplicated for the lay brothers, who ate in part of the west range undercroft, partitioned also to form a large store, so they did not enjoy its long vista of a complete double-bay quadripartite vault, with ribs rising continuously from central piers. Above was their dormitory, and at the south end their reredorter, built over the canalised River Skell, like an arcaded public convenience. Their

infirmary was also built over the water, on a wide bridge. To its north-west were guest ranges, with flue blocking a circular window, above two round-headed first-floor windows, formerly of two lights.

19

Gisborough Priory, Cleveland
12th–14th century

NZ 618163. Guisborough. Accessed from A171 Whitby–Guisborough road

[A] EH

The entrance to the priory is a discreet wall door beside the parish church of St Nicholas, which lay within the precinct. Further west the late 12th-century gatehouse has a rolled outer arch, round and wide above half-octagonal chamfered responds, inner wall with two arches, one elliptical, and vaulted carriageway. A nearby length of precinct wall has mural chambers.

A well-endowed house of Augustinian canons, founded by Robert de Brus early in the 12th century, destruction after Dissolution in 1539 was thorough here, but most buildings other than the gate were rebuilt in the mid-13th century. However, soon after completion of the new church, a plumber soldering lead on the roof in 1289 accidentally set it on fire. What does remain is therefore of the Decorated period.

The main fragment, the east presbytery wall, is of high quality, the window jambs richly moulded, with leafy carving and shields. It illustrates well the three-dimensional planning of such a great church. Flanking the gaping hole of the vast east window are deep stepped buttresses, to resist the thrust of the arcades, the springing for which survives.

Corner buttresses, that to the south panelled and traceried and with crocketed image niches, have crocketed turrets, and contained spiral staircases up to the aisle parapets. Passages, with small windows over the aisle east windows, led above the aisle vaults to the triforium galleries. More stairs in the central buttresses led to the clerestories, and gave access to the space above the presbytery vault, and to the roof. The roof-space gable window has five lights divided 2:1:2 and Geometric tracery.

In the presbytery are coffins and grave covers. Separating the site from the view beyond is a roll-coped ha-ha with ferocious-looking wrought-iron spikes. Behind a garden wall to the south are carved stones, many with masons' marks – window tracery, vaulting ribs and bosses, Early English dog-tooth fragments. Towers at the west end of the church are represented by the base of a very large quatrefoil pier. A passage south of the cellarer's range west of the cloister has quadripartite vaulting.

Against a backdrop of conifers on the Cleveland Hills can be seen the priory's octagonal two-stage dovecote, a cupola above its pyramidal roof, within the glorious palette of a market garden which perhaps inspires this particularly well-tended monument to emulation.

In the parish church is a chest tomb from the priory, of the 1520s, very large, with polished top and richly carved sides. Instead of weeping angels, trefoil-headed niches house knights holding Brus shields, between niched piers containing more figures. The west end is lost, but facing east is the seated prior and canons praying to a seated Virgin.

20

Jervaulx Abbey, N Yorkshire
12th–15th century

SE 171857. East Witton, on A6108 Leyburn–Ripon road, 5 miles (8 km) SE of Leyburn

[A]

This privately owned site, as important for botanical heritage as monastic remains, is set in sheep-grazed parkland. East of the access path is the abbey gatehouse, part-ruin, part-cottage. Later gateways, to an 18th- and 19th-century

Gisborough Priory, looking east. EH

Jervaulx Abbey, west wall of dorter. JH

domestic and farm complex, stand to the west. At the entrance, the visitor notices fragments beside the honesty box, including a bench-end from the chapter house, and the infirmary laying-out slab, with drainage channel and candle placements.

Jervaulx, a Cistercian house established in 1156, retains much Transitional work, of beautiful honey-coloured squarish rectangular sandstone ashlars. Visitors pass the undercroft of the lay brothers' range and go through a short sub-reredorter tunnel, ducking beneath a tree, to the church. The night stair descends to the Transitional south-west door. Lining the sides of the once-vaulted aisled nave are pieces of moulded ribs, window tracery, wall-arcade gablets and quatrefoils, dog-tooth window surrounds and shaft capitals.

Among medieval floor slabs is the grave cover of Brian Askarth, one of the monks of the abbey, with floriate cross-head and priest's chalice containing the Host. The east end of the nave was rebuilt with very graceful piers of eight keeled shafts. The ornate wooden screen which separated the lay brothers' nave from monks' choir survives in Aysgarth parish church (NY). A weathered effigy lies beside the raised choir stalls platform. The transepts had east aisles, and a stone altar slab, broken but with five consecration crosses visible, is in the north-east chapel. Another altar base

remains in the south transept. Stone coffins lie in the once-vaulted east choir chapels.

A reconstructed fragment of paired-shaft arcade may be found in the cloister, where the east side had four round-arched openings, as at Fountains (18, NY). Windows, roll-moulded outside and in, flanked the doorway to the chapter house, which has perimeter benches, and more grave covers. Six monolithic columns with stiff-leaf capitals carried its vaulting, which sprang from wall corbels with short, triple shafts, filleted and with banded capitals. The thrust was resisted by external buttresses with chamfered bases.

Dominating the domestic ranges is the tall meat kitchen, with two vast fireplaces and very large south window. It reflects not only the less austere 15th-century monastic lifestyle, but the provision of more luxurious food for corrodians, who used surplus abbey accommodation. Other buildings show evidence of alterations made for them: the extensive infirmary range at the east end of the complex (which has original Geometric windows) has 15th-century shouldered doorways, and windows of five-cusped lights with sunken spandrels. Sub-division into apartments can be seen at the north end of the monks' dormitory. Above another vaulted undercroft, this has evenly

spaced lancet windows which were shuttered, but show no evidence of glazing. Between their splayed interior openings are scars of wooden screens which seem to have formed cubicles.

21

Kirkham Priory, N Yorkshire
12th–14th century

SE 735657. Westow, on minor road S of A64, 5 miles (8 km) SW of Malton

[A] EH

Traffic hurtles to the coast on the A64, but the York–Scarborough railway takes a scenic route, inoffensively passing close to the lovely site in the wooded valley of the River Derwent, which is crossed by a fine old bridge. Seen first is a medieval cross-base with small square steps, two quatrefoils on each side, and the stump of the shaft.

Kirkham's late 13th-century gatehouse still greets visitors nobly, a wide single arch, set in crocketed and panel-traceried gable. Above are five first-floor gablets, two containing stellar-traceried windows, and a plethora of heraldic shields, sculpted figures and fabulous beasts. Large vaulted ranges flanked the gatehouse.

The priory was founded by Augustinian canons in the 1120s. The plain aisleless nave of the 1140s has remained little altered, except for the external twin west towers which were added in the 1170s. The east-end plan became more complex in the early 13th century when the choir was rebuilt with eight bays and vaulted aisles. Several members of the de Roos family, Lords of Helmsley Castle (47, NY) and patrons of the priory, were buried here. A small part of the east end stands to a good height, its lancet windows with stiff-leaf decoration. In the 14th century chapels were added to the north and south. There are several grave covers, one in the north transept with wheel-head cross, another with a matrix for a brass.

The prior's accommodation and infirmary lay to the north-east of the church. The main drain, beautifully masoned, continued into the reredorter,

Kirkham Priory, the gatehouse. EH

cusped flanking cinque-cusped, two five-foil circles and one of four in Geometric tracery above.

22

Monk Bretton Priory, S Yorkshire
12th–15th century

SE 373065. Barnsley. 1 mile (1.6 km) E of town centre, off A633

[A] EH

More accessible by service buses than many abbey ruins, this is Barnsley: the brown sandstone walls are soot-blackened, but the custodians' welcome is as warm as if coal fires were burning in all the rooms. Founded rather unusually as a Cluniac monastery in 1154, it switched to the Benedictines in the late 13th century, after lengthy disputes over priors' appointments. Some of the buildings also differ from the familiar monastic pattern.

The wide early 15th-century gatehouse, with image niche above its arched opening, has first-floor flat-headed windows of two cinque-cusped lights, and a small remaining section of crenellation. West of the carriageway was a heated porter's room, and the almonry to the east now contains carved stones. A Tudor-arched doorway on the inside face leads to a stair tower. Across to the east is a detached two-storey building of *c*.1300, perhaps used for administrative purposes, the valley of its double-pitched roof internally supported on monolithic medieval columns. Outside this building are two large dish-like receptacles, each formed from a single gritstone block, probably used for pressing fruit or grains for their juices.

Grave covers intersperse stone floor slabs in the aisled nave; the transepts had east chapels. In the south side of the aisleless presbytery is the pulpit entrance. The chapter house, east of the rather small cloister, has two good grave covers. In the refectory are two unequal Geometric south windows; to its south-east the deep drain of the reredorter, flushed by a leat from the monastic corn water-mill.

connected to the first-floor dorter by round-arched doorways apparently planned on the 'in' and 'out' principle. A large and rather plain chapter house lay to the north of the cloister, which still gives a sense of sheltered enclosure. Along, rather than projecting from, its east side, the 13th-century frater was entered by a re-used late 12th-century round-arched doorway, rather small but richly ornamented. A spiral staircase led to the south-west corner of its under-croft, which had vaulting resting on five-sided columns with nail-head capitals.

One hopes the canons had very clean hands, for the two-bay lavatorium in the south-east cloister corner is sumptuous. Each moulded pointed arch has three-bay blind tracery on the rear wall, triple-

Monk Bretton Priory, the prior's accommodation. EH

The west range accommodated the prior on the first floor, where there is a very fine 14th-century fireplace, its stone hood tapering from an embattled lintel, supported on shafted jambs, with small shelves for lamps projecting from each side. A large inserted arch represents a 15th-century extension and upgrading of the prior's suite, and this comfortable range was kept in residential use after the Dissolution. A 17th-century gatehouse was added to it, with chamfered elliptical arches which rise from cornice capitals forming wide carriage and narrower pedestrian openings, those to the south with labels.

23

Mount Grace Priory, N Yorkshire
15th–17th century

SE 453982. Osmotherley, on A19, 7 miles (11.2 km) NE of Northallerton

[A] EH and NT

Best preserved of English Charterhouses, Mount Grace provides a tranquil haven just off the busy A19 road, only the tower against a backdrop of wooded hillside drawing attention to its presence. The Carthusians arrived here in 1398. Their unusual conventual plan is clearly seen here. The communal buildings form a range separating two asymmetrical quadrangles. Around the great court are the monks' cells, actually spacious two-storey cottages: more mundane storage, domestic and lay brothers' accommodation surrounded the lesser court, into which the once-vaulted gatehouse led.

The range to its west became the post-Dissolution house, remodelled by Thomas Lascelles, the tower porch dated *1652* in the door spandrels. The mansion has an oak staircase with symmetrically turned balusters on both sides of the flights, several chamfered fireplaces and doorways, some with original doors, and various chamfer-stop mouldings. English Heritage and the National Trust have combined to produce a well-presented display on medieval

Mount Grace Priory. From W Chambers Lefroy, *The Ruined Abbeys of Yorkshire*, 1883.

monasticism. There is also a fitting tribute to Sir Lothian Bell, the early 20th-century owner who appreciated the ruin's importance.

His decision to rebuild a well-preserved cell in the great court would now be controversial but, having inherited it, English Heritage has complemented it by reconstructing the outbuildings and commissioning replica furniture. The result provides a powerful image of a Carthusian's solitary, but otherwise comfortable, life. In the living room is a dining table, linen-fold panelled chair, three-legged stool, and food cupboard with perforated door and panels; in the study a desk for manuscript copying, stool and painted chest; and in the bedroom a tray for a straw pallet, clothes chest and painted altarpiece. In the upper room, used for practical occupations, are a loom, spinning wheel, trestle table, and a storage chest carved and brightly painted in medieval colours.

Coats of arms over the cell doors unsurprisingly testify to the order's upper-class appeal. That the life was not only luxurious but exceedingly solitary is amply shown by the provision beside each door of an angled hatch, through which food could be delivered to the occupant without his seeing the servant

in the pentice, the large roof corbels of which remain.

Mount Grace gives particular pleasure to those who relish monastic drainage arrangements, as both output and input are exceptionally well preserved. Behind each cell was a garden, in the perimeter wall of which a *necessarium* projected out over a drain, cleverly designed to take advantage of the fall of the site, picking up from each cell in succession. On the hillside in the north-east corner is a delightful little building sheltering one of the springs serving the priory. This spring overflows into the drain.

The provision of spacious quarters limited the number of monks to about twenty-five. Thus the shared buildings are small, and were not in daily use. Only on festivals were meals taken in the refectory, beside the door of which is the small lavatorium, with scars of water and drainage pipes. Nearby was the prior's apartment, with a first-floor oriel window to see what was happening in all corners of the great court – presumably myopic candidates for the post were rejected.

The aisleless nave of the church, with west door off the lesser court, is very small, the intention apparently being to discourage visitors. Two added chapels resemble transepts. That the crossing tower was slotted into a pre-existing church can be seen from straight masonry joints: its staircase wall bears many masons' marks. In the monks' choir is a small area of encaustic tiles, and round the sides are stone foundations for their wooden choir stalls.

24

Nun Monkton Priory Church, N Yorkshire
12th–13th century

SE 511579. Nun Monkton. 2 miles (3.2 km) N of A59 York–Harrogate road, 8 miles (12.8 km) W of York. At E end of village

[A]

Nun Monkton is a fine village, its large green with pond and maypole, and its pub sensibly named after a racehorse, Alice Hawthorn. A private-looking avenue at the east end leads to the parish church and its neighbours – a house of c.1670 with superb wood-carving, and a small house with rare rusticated 17th-century brickwork. A beautiful weeping beech tree almost shrouds the west elevation of St Mary's Church, originally the nave of the priory founded c.1153 by Benedictine nuns who endowed the village with its name, and the region with its finest remaining nunnery.

The lower half of the west front of the church, dating from about a generation post-foundation, has typically Romanesque masonry. The five-order doorway, in pelleted gabled portal, is flanked by two bays of statue recesses, round-arched and roll-moulded, with water-leaf capitals to shafts – here, one statue and part of another survive. The end bays project slightly to strengthen the corners of the building.

Construction apparently stopped for about sixty years, for above are three fully Early English lancet windows, stepped in height and with dog-tooth jambs and ringed shafts. A belfry tower rises from the gable. The north and south walls have nail-head labels over smaller lancets, a sill band, corbel table and pilaster buttresses. There are two

south doors. The east end dates from the restoration of 1873, and its windows contain superb stained glass by William Morris.

Inside the church, the tower is supported on square piers, the organ now suspended between them. Several medieval grave covers at the west end include some of prioresses. The Romanesque lower walls are thick and plain, the Early English upper walls thinner and set back to the outside, forming a gallery level with the sills of the windows, which therefore seem high and nunnery-like. There is large nail-head enrichment, and shafts divide the gallery front into bays of arched niches, wider by the windows, narrower between. The effect is impressive, and the shafting clearly shows that vaulting was intended. In the floor below the present altar is the medieval altar slab, with five consecration crosses.

25

Rievaulx Abbey, N Yorkshire
12th–13th century

SE 577849. Rievaulx, 2¼ miles (3.6 km) W of Helmsley, off B1257

[A] EH

The Rye valley is here so narrow that the standard monastic plan would only fit in if swung round so that the liturgical east end of the church actually faced east-south-east. Rievaulx was the first Yorkshire Cistercian abbey, founded in 1131 from Clairvaux itself, with St Bernard's secretary as first abbot. It was the mission centre for an ambitious programme of increasing religious purity in the north of England, and rapidly became one of the largest Cistercian houses, with 140 monks, 240 lay brothers, plus at least as many lesser

St Mary's Church, Nun Monkton, lower part of the west front. RCHME

Rievaulx Abbey, the crossing and east end of the church. JB

members. These numbers are reflected in its size.

The first main building phase occurred during the mid-12th-century abbacy of Aelred. The square piers of the lay brothers' nave, which was very large and rather austere, date from this time. The lower storeys of the transepts are contemporary and Romanesque in style but their tops, in different stone, show they were raised when design had moved into the Early English period, c.1225. The choir was completely rebuilt in the same building phase, being completed c.1240.

The choir, again large, and standing to its full height, is a superb example of Cistercian Early English architecture. Each arcade bay consists of a richly moulded pointed arch on piers modelled into shafting and turned into diagonals in plan, to make them look more delicate. The triforium has paired arches, each subdivided into two. Twin

windows are set back behind a pointed arch which encloses the clerestory walkway. There is much dog-tooth and nail-head enrichment. The roof was vaulted, and on the north side are two complete flying buttresses which formed part of the structural system of the vaulting. It is also interesting to compare the inner visible elevations of the arcade walls with the outer elevations.

On the south side of the main cloister the almost complete refectory was also rebuilt in Early English style and must have been one of the finest examples of its kind. The chapter house east of the cloister had an apsidal end. To its south is a secondary cloister which served the infirmary quarters, unusually large here because of the high numbers present. Late in the abbey's time, when numbers had diminished, parts of these buildings were converted into a luxurious apartment for the abbot.

26
Roche Abbey, S Yorkshire
12th–14th century

SK 544898. 1½ miles (2.4 km) S of Maltby and S of A634

[A] EH

Below the cliff of beautiful white magnesian limestone, quarried for the buildings of this Cistercian house which was founded in 1147, so spectacular is the site of Roche Abbey that it was incorporated into the mid-18th-century landscape designed for nearby Sandbeck Park by 'Capability' Brown, architect of the pretty Gothick cottage which serves as entrance kiosk.

Visitors to the abbey first pass through the late 13th-century gatehouse, square in plan, with outer and inner triple-chamfered pointed arches, and a cross-wall with pedestrian

29

and vehicle arches. Lining through with the vehicle arch both fore and aft are quadripartite vault bays, with chamfered ribs and neatly masoned webs, flanked by smaller narrower vault bays on the outside, and unvaulted compartments inside. The start of a north newel staircase has beside it a pointed-arched candle-niche.

The inner east walls of the transepts with east aisles stand to their full height, and show English Cistercian church design at a very interesting stage. It is almost fully Gothic, but of only *c*.1170, an earlier date than might be expected, so a certain amount of experimentation is evident. On each side are two arcade bays, the arches sadly now weathering at an alarming rate. Their three orders rest on business-like shafts with water-leaf capitals. Over each arch are two rather severe triforium-level blind arches: above, as if the Gothic effort hitherto has been too exhausting, are single round-arched clerestory windows.

Here the vaulting ribs sprang from a shaft carried up from the pier, but a refinement of detail at an advanced constructional stage required the shaft to be tripled above the clerestory sill band. The foundations of the choir, presumably begun fractionally earlier, did not envisage vaulting at all, for

shafting there was hastily corbelled out from the triforium sill, and again tripled higher up.

The chancel was altered in the 14th century – its multi-canopied sedilia must have been a fine feature – but 12th-century details include the cloister doorway, round-arched with continuous slight chamfer, and label to the inside, the arch becoming a blind tympanum on the outside. There were apparently fewer lay brothers here than at many Cistercian houses, for almost half the nave was given over to the choir monks. The domestic buildings south of the church display a particularly adventurous drainage plan, with numerous bridges.

27
St Mary's Church, Lastingham, N Yorkshire
11th, 13th and 19th century

SE 727904. Lastingham, 3½ miles (5.6 km) N of A170 Helmsley–Pickering road

[A]

The Venerable Bede recorded the foundation of the 7th-century Northumbrian monastery here by

The crypt, St Mary's Church, Lastingham. RCHME

Ethelwald, son of King Oswald, and of four brothers, all priests, who between them produced three bishops and two saints, Cedd and Chad. The only physical remains are some carved stones, but the present church on the site seems particularly hallowed by its ancient sanctity.

Of sandstone of almost ashlar quality, with squat west tower, tall aisled nave, and shorter chancel, it has, promisingly, an apse with corbel table, pilaster buttresses and three round-arched windows set rather high above the ground. The church is substantially that of the monastery rebuilt in 1078 by Stephen, Abbot of Whitby, with a contemporary, rather than an earlier, crypt. His work seems even more impressive as the monks abandoned Lastingham in 1086 and moved to York.

Despite their contemporaneous relationship, it is logical as well as tempting to visit the crypt first. Its square plan has a three-bay nave with aisles, each bay groin-vaulted, and a barrel-vaulted east apse. The unchamfered round arches between the bays rest on short circular piers with large capitals of a variety of designs. A staircase in the north aisle provided the original access, from outside the church.

In the aisles are antiquarian items, from the first monastery a small circular window, and a dragon's head perhaps from the bishop's throne. Also of pre-Conquest date are shafts and heads of important Anglian crosses, including one of exceptional size, and a hogback tombstone. There are also medieval grave covers, and decorated timber wall-

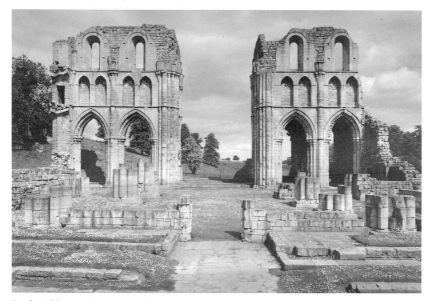

Roche Abbey, pulpitum, choir and transepts from the west. EH

plates, two carved with dragons, one with rosettes. An old bier is thought to be of pre-Reformation date.

Ascending to the main church, the apse windows have inner round arches on colonnettes, their capitals with simple curled volutes, and a piscina has a scalloped basin. A wide round arch, with roll-moulding, on shafts, frames the apse, then comes a single barrel-vaulted bay with similar west arch, completing the original sanctuary. The present nave was intended as a large square chancel with aisles, and the bay to its west as the crossing of a cruciform church. Only the main piers of that plan date from the 11th century: the double-bay arcades, of Early English double-chamfered pointed arches on quatrefoil piers, were inserted when this became a parish church in 1228. The impressive groin vault dates from J L Pearson's sympathetic 19th-century restoration. The aisles have 16th-century bench seats. Near the simple round-arched south door is a very substantial pedestal stoup.

Outside the church on the west wall, now flanking the Perpendicular tower, but intended to be inside the church just west of the crossing, are the responds of the nave arcade. In the village, picturesquely in a slight hollow of the North York Moors, clear water still flows into St Cedd's Well. At nearby Spaunton, the medieval manorial court leet survives and still sits.

28

Thornton Abbey, Humberside
13th–16th century

TA 115190. On minor road 2 miles (3.2 km) ENE of Thornton Curtis, a village on A1077 Barton-upon-Humber–Ulceby road. On S side of Humber estuary, 2 miles (3.2 km) SE of Barrow upon Humber

[A] EH

William le Gros, Count of Aumale, Lord of Holderness and (after the Battle of the Standard), Earl of Yorkshire, founded this house of Augustinian canons in 1139, and was buried here in 1180. The buildings show it was a prosperous

Thornton Abbey, exterior of the gatehouse. HMK

house, apparently historically incident-free until after its surrender in 1539 when it was, unusually, refounded in 1541 by Henry VIII as a college of secular canons. This was suppressed again by Edward VI in 1548.

Major rebuilding began *c*.1264. Of the church only picked-out foundations remain, but the nave had a double west door and octagonal piers on square bases. There are several grave covers, many with good lettering: one in the north transept has a figure incised as on a brass. The choir columns have square foundations, and an aisleless but vaulted Lady Chapel was added to the east end in the late 14th century.

The transepts had east aisles. The south transept south-east chapel south wall survives almost complete, with piscina and blind window with Geometric tracery. Attached to its back are two walls of the octagonal chapter house, with slightly later blind Geometric tracery. The chapter house was approached by a four-bay vestibule, north of which the parlour is a still rib-vaulted corridor with sitting bays. More seating remains in the north-west corner of the cloister, which again was vaulted. In the cloistral buildings are a few decorated floor tiles.

The main glory of Thornton Abbey is its gatehouse, in very early pale brown

brick with stone dressings. Its crenellations were licensed in 1382, but the fortifications are reminiscent of a Gothick folly, particularly the 16th-century outer barbican, an avenue of arcaded wings with arrow slits and end turrets. The gatehouse itself has three bays divided by projecting turrets, through which a walkway passes, carried on a cusped pelmet-like support over the richly moulded archway. Above are canopied niches, some still with figures.

Benches line the carriageway, which has a portcullis slot, multi-rib vaulting, and original inner wooden doors. The inside elevation has a first-floor oriel window, and four five-sided projecting turrets: one contains a spiral staircase leading to the flat roof, which becomes progressively steeper, and has a delightful vault at the top.

The gatehouse contained splendid quarters, probably for the abbot. The main first-floor room, with a display of architectural fragments, has a very large fireplace, corbels to the floor above decorated with figures, and the oriel has a piscina. In side chambers are floor tiles and a garderobe. The top-floor room has similar facilities, and the staircase doorway is Tudor-arched with a deep roll. The middle arch of three along the west side contains a hole for the portcullis mechanism.

31

Places of Worship

The region is rich in fine churches, and important examples (particularly those not normally open) have reluctantly had to be excluded for reasons of space. An entire book would need to be devoted to the places of worship in the region in order to do justice to them. A few of the churches not included are mentioned below, to give visitors more of a rounded view and point them towards yet further treasures. The aim in this chapter is to spread coverage both chronologically and geographically.

The cathedrals at **York** (44, NY) and **Ripon** (33, NY) alone provide a variety of architectural history. The immense volume of York Minster offers a Romanesque crypt, Early English transepts, Decorated nave and Perpendicular choir – plus Roman remains. Ripon has an early Saxon crypt, a fine Early English west front, Romanesque, Transitional, Decorated and Perpendicular features, and its 15th-century choir stalls provide an appropriate monument to the Ripon school of wood-carvers. Excellent choir stalls also survive in the delightful Beverley Minster (80, H), included in chapter 7.

The era of pre-edifice secular Christian worship is noted in the pre-Conquest crosses from Easby (17, NY) in chapter 2 and Leeds (88, WY) in chapter 7. Pre-Conquest survivals notably include a complete church at **Kirk Hammerton** (38, NY); a probable two-thirds of the church, including an excellent tower, at **Barton-upon-Humber** (42, H); and a nave and wonderfully descriptive sundial in the delightful setting of **Kirkdale** (36, NY).

The unique Romanesque crypt and church at Lastingham (27, NY) are included in chapter 2. Highlights of the Vale of York's series of fine Norman churches (all in the southern tip of North Yorkshire) are the complete Romanesque apsidal church at Birkin, and the churches at Sherburn-in-Elmet and Stillingfleet (the latter also has interesting later work).

Gothic churches are numerous in the region. **Skelton** (35, NY), near York, provides an Early English gem, cathedral-like in quality, parochial in scale, and even complete. **St Hilda, Hartlepool** (37, C) is on a much larger scale. Humberside astonishes with the grandeur and richness of its churches, particularly of the Decorated and Perpendicular periods, such as **Howden** (29, H), **Patrington** (40, H), and St Mary, Beverley (80, H). Hedon would have been included except that it is normally locked, in an area where this is unusual. Several churches are mentioned in chapter 7, and two medieval chantry chapels are included in chapter 8.

Post-Reformation ecclesiastical work

(*Left*) St Patrick, Patrington. ES

(*Right*) Ripon Cathedral, misericord showing a mermaid.

is represented by the rural private chapel at **Red House** (32, NY), and the urban example of St John, Briggate is mentioned in chapter 7 (88, WY). The same gazetteer entry also includes the early 18th-century Holy Trinity, Boar Lane; and of similar date is the fine parish church at Stockton-on-Tees (C). The splendid Turner Mausoleum at **Kirkleatham church** (34, C) is the work of James Gibbs, and at Horbury (WY) the visitor may see that great northern architect John Carr's own monumental church. Briefly described are Holy Trinity, York (44, NY) and St Mary, Whitby (94, NY), both with examples of Georgian church fittings, which seem quaint to those whose mental picture of a proper church has been over-influenced by 19th-century restorers.

The great Victorian period of church building is represented here by one sole example, Burges's rural **St Mary, Studley Royal** (39, NY) – his similar edifice at Skelton-on-Ure is briefly noted under Newby Hall (74, NY). Scott's All Souls', Haley Hill is mentioned in chapter 7 under Halifax (84, WY), and his fine urban parish church at Doncaster (SY) is worth a visit. The outstandingly fine 19th-century church of St Martin is included under Scarborough (93, NY), and Butterfield's town church in a country village at Baldersby St James (NY) is also highly recommended.

Twentieth-century church building is illustrated by George Pace's inspiring chapel at Scargill in Wharfedale (NY) and the new Roman Catholic Cathedral of the Middlesbrough Diocese (C).

Churches are those of the established church unless otherwise stated. The visitor may sample nonconformism at the **Quaker Meeting House, Countersett** (31, NY) in Wensleydale, the **Upper Independent Chapel, Heckmondwike** (43, WY) and Ignatius Bonomi's Roman Catholic masterpiece, **St Paulinus, Brough Park** (41, NY), near Catterick. Mentioned elsewhere are York's Centenary Methodist and Unitarian chapels (95, NY), Scarborough's Westborough Methodist Church (93, NY) and the splendid Congregational Church at Saltaire (106, WY).

The region boasts an abundance of

St Mary, Studley Royal, from the south-west. RCHME

churches worth visiting for their contents, including Methley (WY) with its fine monuments, one even in a chantry niche. The visitor's itinerary should also include the splendid alabaster monuments at Harewood (72, WY); and Whitkirk (79, WY) has fine memorials of several periods. Church monuments are also described in Skipton (59, NY), Coxwold (82, NY) and Ripley (91, NY), as are the medieval wrought ironwork over the Marmion tomb at West Tanfield (58, NY), and the fine medieval screen at Flamborough (104, H). Wall-paintings in Easby and Pickering churches can be found under Easby Abbey (17, NY) and Pickering Castle (50, NY). Some of York's vast wealth of medieval stained glass is included under York Minster (44, NY).

Some of my decisions have unashamedly been made on the doubtful grounds of access: many favourite churches are usually locked, others have been eliminated because they are not readily accessible, and keys (to Cleveland churches in particular) where available to visitors, are not often easily obtained. It is largely a geographical matter, in that Cleveland and West and South

Yorkshire churches tend to be locked, and those in North Yorkshire and Humberside are more likely to be open. Friday is a good day to attempt access to locked churches, as they are often open for cleaning and flower arranging.

29

Howden Minster, Humberside
14th–15th century

SE 748282. Howden, near M62 junction 37 and 9 miles (14.4 km) SE of Selby on A63(T). In town centre

[A]

This small-scale market town is a gem, predominantly of brick, with narrow streets of mainly Georgian buildings. In the Market Place the 1909 cross sits on old circular steps. Nearby is Howden Minster, a collegiate church which belonged to the Bishop and Cathedral of Durham, who in the early 14th century rebuilt it, Decorated and cruciform, beginning with the nave. A late 14th-century octagonal chapter house was added south of the now-ruined choir, also an early 15th-century lantern crossing tower, on which another stage was put later that century, and a grammar school was added to the west end of the south nave aisle c.1500. The east front was particularly rich, as it had a large window flanked by stepped buttresses with tiers of image niches (more were also in the gable above) and five crowning turrets.

Inside, six-bay nave arcades of almost Perpendicular design have keeled pier shafts, and clerestories with walkways immediately above the arches. The Decorated octagonal font has blind nodding ogee tracery, an old chest appropriately collects donations, and in the floor are many fine incised grave slabs. East of the crossing a magnificent 15th-century pulpitum has a loft with pierced parapet, crocketed ogee canopy, central continuously moulded four-centred archway with quatrefoils and flanking steeply canopied niches with old statues.

At the crossing the tower ceiling is of

1930, the south-west pier has a 14th-century statue of the Virgin with dove on her shoulder, and in the floor a 15th-century memorial brass. In the south transept east aisle a crocketed wall niche with traceried back contains a tomb chest. Its two recumbent effigies are perhaps Sir John Metham (died 1311) and his wife: he with crossed legs and enviable curls; her legs crossed, in the opposite direction, under folded drapery, her head within a canopy. A free-standing chest tomb with weepers in trefoiled niches supports an effigied knight in chain mail, perhaps Sir Peter Saltmarshe (died 1338). In the floor are elaborately inscribed slabs, and propped against a wall is the parish coffin of 1664.

South-east of the minster survives the hall of the Bishop of Durham's Palace, much altered with inserted floor and Georgian sashes: the south elevation shows it had three bays. On the kitchen side of the west screens passage is a mixture of old brickwork and stone doorways. From the neater Georgian north front projects the medieval vaulted two-storey porch. Here, the arms of Walter Skirlaw, Bishop of Durham 1388–1405 appear in an elaborate niche in the battlemented

Howden Minster, interior of the chapter house. RCHME

parapet, above a flat-headed traceried window with two cinque-cusped lights and a moulded round archway.

30
Methodist Chapel, Heptonstall, W Yorkshire
18th century

SD 988281. Heptonstall, on minor road ½ mile (0.8 km) N of Hebden Bridge. Off Northgate

[D]

Heptonstall, a quaint hilltop settlement to which access is difficult for vehicles has, mercifully, avoided yellow lines and, instead, comprehensive parking restrictions affect the narrow stone-setted lanes. The millstone grit buildings are almost all of the hand-powered woollen cloth industry era, for up here there was no water power for large Industrial Revolution mills.

Instead there is Weavers' Square, Cloth Hall, and many 17th-, 18th- and 19th-century clothiers' houses. The Grammar School of 1642, now a museum, is in the churchyard of the ruined medieval St Thomas à Becket Church, which partly collapsed in an 1847 storm and was replaced by the present Perpendicular-style church, of St Thomas the Apostle, completed in 1854.

John Wesley paid sixteen visits to Heptonstall, and five times preached in the old parish church, the ugliest he knew, he said. In 1764 he laid the foundation stone of the Methodist Chapel, one of the oldest still in use. It is often referred to as the Octagon, for that centralised plan-form was considered by Wesley to provide better acoustics for preaching than the conventional axial plan of a typical medieval parish church, as it placed all the congregation within a relatively short distance of the pulpit.

In fact, however, the chapel is hexagonal, with two sides longer than the others. The main disadvantage of the plan is that it is difficult to extend, a problem which faced the Heptonstall Wesleyan Society in 1802, when the building was lengthened and raised in

Methodist Chapel, Heptonstall. W LYNCH

height to provide a gallery on slender Tuscan columns. Another problem is roofing and, according to tradition, Wesley commissioned the Heptonstall roof from carpenters in Rotherham (SY), where there was already an octagonal chapel, and they prefabricated the roof and transported it over the moors by horses.

Large quoins articulate the angles of the building, a horizontal band divides the elevations into two storeys, the upper windows being smaller and rectangular in shape, while those on the main storey are round-arched, with Tuscan capitals and tripartite keystones in their ashlar surrounds.

31
Quaker Meeting House, Countersett, N Yorkshire
18th century

SD 919879. Countersett, in Wensleydale, 3 miles (4.8 km) SW of Askrigg and S of A684 Hawes–Aysgarth road

[A]

In the region's remote upland areas the established church was under-represented, and alternative religious groups attracted much support, but their followers were mostly poor, and generally left little architectural evidence of their worship. Countersett Meeting House is an important exception. The 'Quakers' (as they became known) were among the earliest nonconformists, and their founder,

Quaker Meeting House, Countersett. RCHME/CS

George Fox, visited Wensleydale in 1652 and 1677.

The first Quaker in the area was Richard Robinson (1628–93), a yeoman of great ability. In 1650 he and his wife Margaret extensively altered their home, now called Countersett Hall, then consisting of a hall-house and service room with lofts above. They inserted fine mullioned windows, added a dated two-storey porch, large panelled parlour with spacious bedroom above (both with segmental-arched fireplaces), and improved other first-floor rooms, putting a trefoil-headed fire-window in that over the hall.

Quaker meetings were held in the hall from 1652, and George Fox stayed there on his 1677 tour. Richard suffered severe penalties during Quaker persecutions of the 1660s and 1670s, but after the granting of partial toleration, his house was formally registered and licensed as a meeting house in 1689.

In 1710 Richard and Margaret's eldest son, Michael, built a separate Meeting House, a simple rectangular building in local rubble stone with stone flag roof. Since loving restoration in 1977, it gives a convincing impression of having remained unchanged from construction, but has in fact been altered several times. In 1732 an upper

floor was inserted, then lowered in 1778 when the present three large sash front windows were inserted. The Primitive Methodists shared the chapel for about a century from 1872, and installed a pulpit, now removed. Many 18th-century pine interior fittings, however, remain: fielded panelling, elders' bench, ministers' gallery, and simple loose benches.

The Quakers have a good record for providing educational facilities, and in 1772 they built a Countersett school-room on the first floor above the stabling – the latter being always in short supply when people travelled long distances in remote locations.

32

Red House Chapel, Moor Monkton, N Yorkshire
17th century

SE 529571. N of A59 York–Harrogate road, ½ mile (0.8 km) towards Moor Monkton then 2 miles (3.2 km) E along lane to Red House [A]

Royalist Sir Henry Slingsby's diary provides graphic details of the Siege of

York and Battle of Marston Moor in 1644. His father and namesake, in the 17th century's first quarter, built what is now a school chapel. In brick with stone quoins and surrounds to openings, and Westmorland slate roof, it is externally rather plain. The north side gives no hint that this is a chapel, but the east window has three lights and almost Perpendicular tracery. The south side has two tiers of windows, of three cinque-cusped lights above, two-light with ovolo mullions below. Above the round-arched west doorway a terracotta panel has a pious inscription.

The dark oak fittings of the panelled interior are complete. The nave, occupying rather less than half the space, has relatively plain pews: beyond the two-tier screen with convex square-section balusters and paired doors are benches with ornately carved ends and poppy-head finials. Below the east window painted glass, by Baernard Dinninckhoff of York, the communion table is railed with short enriched balusters and bow-fronted gate. The pulpit has arcaded panels with inverted pilasters.

The west gallery is reached by a splendid staircase with symmetrical balusters on both sides, and enriched newel posts topped by huge finials of a short downward-tapering and ornamented 'column' below an entablature. Each is inscribed with the name of a Yorkshire gentry family – Slingsby, plus Cumberland, Fairfax, Fauconberg, Northumberland and Vavasour – and surmounted by the relevant heraldic device, e.g., the Slingsby crest of a lion on a leopard's head. Half-way up sits a lead blackamoor, which once served as a candle-holder.

It seems likely that the staircase was brought out of Red House itself when it was remodelled in 1864, for Sir Henry Slingsby's diary records: 'The staircase was furnished ye last year by John Gowland . . . upon every post a crest is set of my especial friends and of my brothers-in-law, and upon that post yt bears up the half-pace there sits a Blackamore by Andrew Karne.' This Dutchman provided several other sculptures in the area.

Red House Chapel, interior from the west. RCHME

33

Ripon Cathedral, N Yorkshire
7th and 12th–16th century

SE 314711. Ripon, 10 miles (16 km) N of Harrogate on A61. E of Market Place

[A]

Shortly after a monastery was established here *c*.660, St Wilfrid became abbot, and built the surviving crypt, and a church which was destroyed in 950. The foundation became a collegiate church, and rebuilding begun in the late 12th century under Archbishop of York Roger de Pont L'Évêque was completed in the 1220s.

Early 16th century major alterations were halted by the Reformation. The diocese was re-created in 1836, and Ripon parish church became a cathedral. The 1220s west front is particularly fine, with five bays of lancets in two tiers, the upper one stepped, above a triple portal. This indicates the contemporary plan, for the nave was not yet aisled, and the twin towers, barely higher than the gable, provided an impressive screen.

Inside, the tower bays are Early English, but the Perpendicular other five date from the early 16th-century addition of aisles, the clerestories almost directly over the arcades with minimal triforia. Irritatingly lopsided is the west crossing arch, one pier Romanesque, the

other rebuilt for a higher arch, with flanking fragments of Early English wall niches. Beyond, the complete Perpendicular east crossing arch successfully frames the pleasing wooden choir vault. The south aisle west end has two fonts: one Perpendicular, black marble with eight concave sides carved with shields and lozenges; the other, its predecessor, like a paddling pool.

The transepts have east aisles. In the Transitional north transept are a Perpendicular panelled stone pulpit and medieval Markenfield chest tombs (see 57, NY), in the Perpendicular south transept aisle classical monuments. The 15th-century choir screen has restored statues but original doors in transverse-ribbed opening. The choir, aisled from

37

Ripon Cathedral, the crossing. ES

Roger's time, east end altered with Geometric tracery c.1300, has Decorated sedilia and piscina, with nodding ogees, crockets and finials. The choir stalls of 1489–94, with misericords and canopies, are splendid work of the Bromflet family of Ripon carvers.

Below the crossing, St Wilfrid's tiny crypt was designed not for services but for pilgrims visiting relics, with two staircases and entrance passages for circulation flow. Its candle niches, round-arched like the doorways, are particularly evocative. Off the south choir aisle the early 14th-century Lady Chapel, now the Library, has a flat ceiling and straight-headed reticulated windows. The round-arched entrance doorway of c.1200 is Transitional, like the chapter house below, with substantial slightly chamfered ribs springing from slender monolithic round columns, and circular windows.

St Wilfrid is commemorated each first August Saturday with a carnival procession. The Market Place is a formal space, with a classical Town Hall of 1801, and obelisk erected 1781 for the long-serving Ripon MP William Aislabie of Studley Royal (78, NY): from it the Ripon Horn is blown nightly at 9pm. Other delights include a 'listed' cabbies' shelter (an upmarket version of a chicken hut on wheels), a gaslight powered by sewer gas, an early medieval leper hospital chapel, terracotta Art Nouveau Spa Baths and Hotel, and the North Bridge, which is partly of 14th-century date.

34

St Cuthbert and Turner Mausoleum, Kirkleatham, Cleveland
18th century

NZ 594218. Kirkleatham, 7 miles (11.2 km) E of Middlesbrough

[A] Open April–October 2–5pm on Saturdays, Sundays and Bank Holidays

The Turner family, who successfully mined alum from the nearby east coast, a mineral used by the textile industry for

Turner Mausoleum, Scheemakers' statue of Marwood William Turner. RCHME

dyeing, bought the manor of Kirkleatham in 1623, and half a century later began a long programme of benefaction which transformed the settlement. The old church tower was replaced in 1731, and, in 1740, north of its chancel was added James Gibbs's Turner Mausoleum. A Georgian nave and chancel, in ashlar sandstone with round-arched windows, constructed by local builder Robert Corney, but perhaps designed by John Carr of York, were grafted in 1761–3.

The octagonal mausoleum, of banded rustication alternately vermiculated, has exaggerated angle buttresses and an attic storey of circular windows above an inscribed band. From a stepped base on a modillion cornice, a pyramidal roof rises rather heavily from a narrowed neck to an urn finial.

Inside the flat-ceilinged church, four-bay Tuscan colonnades spring incongruously from a height above the original box-pews, the latter having been cut down in the 19th century. In the chancel are a floor slab to Robert Coulthirst (died 1631), and wall monuments to John Turner, sergeant-at-law (died 1688) and John and Elizabeth Turner (c.1670). The

mausoleum is through a Gothick door with open classical pediment above, and up a flight of curving steps. The domed interior is circular, its plaster painted to imitate ashlar. The oculi shed a mysterious light on the three large and four small niches below.

The three large niches contain important monumental statuary. In one, elbow on urn, stands mausoleum builder Cholmley Turner (died 1757), MP for York County in four successive parliaments. He married Jane Marwood: their only son, Marwood William Turner, who died young in Lyons on a 'Grand Tour' in 1739, is commemorated on the external inscription. Cholmley commissioned his son's statue from Peter Scheemakers, and the elegant young man is shown with piles of books. Last of the line, Charles (died 1810), has a sarcophagus with allegorical female figure. In the centre is the free-standing sarcophagus of Sir William Turner (died 1692), Alderman of London and its Lord Mayor in 1669, the son of John, who purchased Kirkleatham.

The churchyard gate-piers are Gibbsian, ashlar with alternate courses of vermiculated rustication, and pedestal skulls and cross-bones. Across the road stood the Turners' Jacobean mansion, Gothicised in 1764–7 by John Carr for Sir Charles Turner, sadly demolished in 1956. All that remain are two Gibbsian gate-piers, some garden features, and a fine classical stable block, partly also by Carr, in brick with sandstone dressings.

Nearby, Sir William Turner's Hospital, founded in 1676, largely rebuilt by his nephew Cholmley in 1742, is a large complex on three sides of a quadrangle, the grand entrance flanked by five-bay quadrants terminating in castellated bastions with loop-holes and gun-ports. Paired doorways give access to the almshouses in long two-storey side ranges, in brick with ashlar dressings, the end bays projecting with Gibbsian doorways below niches containing lead figures of an old woman and an old man. The centre ranges flank the Baroque chapel of 1740, almost certainly also by Gibbs, in ashlar sandstone with a tower porch and sumptuous interior.

The nearby Old Hall Museum was the

Free School, also founded by Sir William but built in 1708–9 by Cholmley. It is in pink brick and brown sandstone, has two storeys plus attic, the main 2:5:2 bay elevation with central segmental-pedimented feature, and seven-bay side elevations. Beyond is a leisure pavilion of 1986, with playground and picnic area, catering for the young in a somewhat different manner from that intended by Sir William.

35

St Giles, Skelton, N Yorkshire
13th century

SE 568565. Skelton, off A19, 3 miles (4.8 km) NW of York

[A]

This complete Early English composition to an almost miniature scale was built *c*.1240 for Walter de Gray, Archbishop of York, using the masons who had built his transepts of York Minster (44, NY), and so is of a higher architectural quality than most village churches. In magnesian limestone, the aisled nave and chancel are unified under one roof, which sweeps down low, a bellcote marking division between nave and chancel. The single lancets, small to north and south, share a nail-head drip-mould with the north and priest's doors; west and east gables, where thin buttresses prop the arcades, have larger lancets, shafted and dog-toothed, and vesicae. The south door, in gabled portal, has several richly moulded orders, with nail-head, dog-tooth, shafts, and unfurling stiff-leaf capitals.

The double-chamfered arcades, larger to the chancel, have quadrilobate piers with pronounced fillets, the capitals a single band of nail-head decoration and a dropped fillet. The keel-section string, with nail-head above and below, follows right round the walls, rising over all openings. Side chapels flanked the chancel: all three had identical fittings, very pretty trefoiled piscina with foliated bowl to right, aumbry to left. The interior ashlar

St Giles, Skelton, from the south-west. RCHME

stonework still clearly shows the tooling left by the claw-ended chisels of the medieval masons, and there are many masons' marks.

36

St Gregory, Kirk Dale, N Yorkshire
11th, 13th and 19th century

SE 677858. Kirk Dale, ½ mile (0.8 km) N of A170 Helmsley–Pickering road

[A]

Dedicated to the Pope who in AD 597 sent Augustine to convert the Anglo-Saxons to Christianity, St Gregory's Minster has a mid-11th-century nave, 13th-century north aisle, and relatively modern west tower, chancel and south porch. The porch is important: it protects the astonishing sundial over the door, with Old English inscription describing how Orm, Gamel's son, rebuilt a ruined church here in the time of King Edward and Earl Tostig; the builder was Hawarth, the priest was Brand. Such rare detailed information enables the nave to be precisely dated to 1055–65, and provides the earliest named Yorkshire parish priest.

Anglian carved stones are built into walls, and the nave has long-and-short west quoins. The small west tower of 1827 is Saxon-like: inside it is Orm's very tall and narrow archway, shafted to the west. The south doorway is shafted too, and similar shafts are reset in the chancel arch. In the chancel is a piscina with scalloped basin, and a piece of oak dated *AD 1633* from the previous roof. Above the vestry door hangs a George II coat of arms dated 1748: the nearby 15th-century carving of the Virgin and Child was probably mutilated at the Reformation.

The three-bay north arcade has one bell-like capital of almost Corinthian design. Between the piers are two high-

St Gregory, Kirk Dale, from the south. BJAW

quality 8th–9th century grave slabs, mounted like chest tombs, one with ornate cross, the other with delicate interlace and a motif on its sides like upside-down tassels. Carved fragments on the north aisle wall bench include Anglo-Scandinavian cross shafts, and tombstones of similar and medieval dates.

37

St Hilda, Hartlepool, Cleveland
12th–13th century

NZ 528337. Hartlepool. On the headland
[C]

Next to the partially Anglo-Saxon church at Hart (which has a pleasing unbuttressed 12th-century tower and in the south chancel wall a late 15th-century relief carving of a warrior in armour with a shield), is a fragment of the medieval manor house of the de Brus lords. Developers of the medieval port at Hartlepool, they built here an impressive Early English church dedicated to St Hilda, who before moving to Whitby (94, NY), was the second abbess of the 7th-century monastery founded here by St Aidan, and destroyed by Danish raiders c.800. In the chancel is the tombstone of one of its nuns, Hildithryth.

The unusual west-end plan gives an unfamiliar appearance – a once-open galilee porch clasped between deep buttresses projecting from the tower's west side. The large tower has flying buttresses to north and south, and walls panelled with deeply modelled lancet arcading. The nave clerestory repeats the theme, each bay having triple lancets (two blind flanking a window), all shafted and with stiff-leaf capitals. The aisle windows are Perpendicular enlargements. Only the south portal of the church is Romanesque in tradition, its round arches extravagantly chevroned.

Inside, the galilee and tower are stone vaulted, the later tower arch strangely profiled, stilted and with

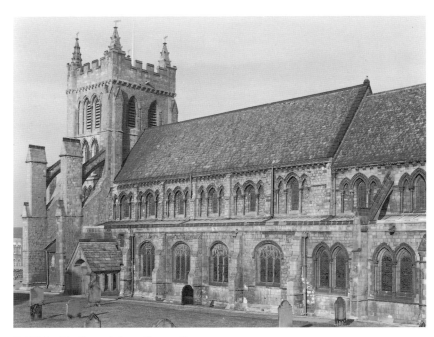

St Hilda, Hartlepool, from the south. RCHME

almost straight arcs. The six-bay nave arcades have octofoil piers, keeled main shafts and simple hollow-profile abaci. Head and sill strings to clerestory windows jut out round single vaulting shafts running up from the arcade capitals to corbels now carrying the roof tie-beams. The aisles have almost

St John the Baptist, Kirk Hammerton, west doorway of tower. BJAW

semicircular transverse arches, resting on corbels on the outer walls.

The splendid richly moulded chancel arch springs from water-leaf capitals. One chancel bay is original, the rest rebuilt by W D Caroe in 1870. There is an east aisle, but none to north or south. In the north nave aisle hangs a 17th-century hatchment to Sir William Blackett, burgess, alderman, and sometime mayor of Newcastle upon Tyne (died 1680).

38

St John the Baptist, Kirk Hammerton, N Yorkshire
Anglo-Saxon and 19th century

SE 465555. Kirk Hammerton, ½ mile (0.8 km) S of A59 Knaresborough–York road
[A]

This complete pre-Conquest church – west tower, nave and chancel – became the south aisle of a larger church tactfully added in 1891 by Charles Hodgson Fowler of Durham. He retained

the existing 13th-century two-bay arcade to link old and new. The Saxon church is built of surprisingly large blocks of stone, and plaster adhering to the nave's south-west corner corroborates the evidence provided by several churches in the Vale of York that some important early buildings were externally plastered. Even larger stones form the quoins of nave and chancel, which probably date from the 8th century. The chancel has two early but post-Saxon south windows. The nave had two south doors, that nearer the east end blocked; the other, forming the church entrance, surrounded by projecting strip-work.

The later, but still pre-Conquest, tower is square and unbuttressed, and has a projecting band below the belfry, which has openings of twin round arches on recessed cylindrical baluster shafts. The west doorway has two orders of regular voussoirs forming a parabolic arch, and somewhat crude shafts in angle recesses.

Inside, the tower arch is slightly horseshoe-shaped and entirely plain. Below the tower is 18th-century panelling and a royal coat of arms. The blocked south nave doorway is internally evident. The chancel arch has two orders and simple stepped imposts. The chancel south wall has a blocked Saxon window above a small sedilia, next to which is a crude 13th-century piscina. The wooden altar rails are early 18th-century, and the altar table perhaps 16th-century, the date of the Dutch reredos above it. The well-proportioned Victorian nave and chancel have pleasing fittings, including rood screen, organ case and panelled reredos. The sanctuary wall paintings are by George Ostrehan, and the east window glass by C E Kempe.

St Mary, Studley Royal, the sanctuary.
RCHME

39
St Mary, Studley Royal, N Yorkshire
19th century

SE 274693. Studley Royal. 2½ miles (4 km) SW of Ripon, S of B6265 Ripon–Pateley Bridge road

[A] EH

From Studley Roger the approach through a screen wall with lodges and gates is along an avenue of lime trees forming a vista between the church and Ripon Cathedral (33, NY), the extremely large spire of the latter facilitating the church's focal role in the Studley Royal landscape. Built in 1871–8 for the first Marquess and Marchioness of Ripon, the High Gothic design is by William Burges.

The interior is breathtaking, but starts relatively quietly in the nave, where black marble shafts contrast with beige stone, and only the central window panels are of coloured glass, the rest grisaille. The patrons' recumbent effigies lie on a large chest tomb at the east end of the south aisle, behind alabaster screens on dark jade green shafts, with wrought ironwork between.

The chancel is an experience of light, colour, spatial effect and great decorative richness. A coloured marble dado with mosaic bands is topped by a gilded band, the horizontality of which contrasts with the verticality of marble shafts in beautiful colours. The windows have two tracery leaves, plate outside, more ornate Decorated bar tracery, almost Moorish, inside: stiff-leaf capitals gilded, tracery stonework stencilled, plaster window reveals painted. Above a plain sedilia bench, the inner tracery shaft is carried on a winged Lion of Judah.

The contemporary stained glass windows, in shapes of bright, pure colours, with little painting, illustrate the Book of Revelation. Angels stand in the inner tracery, also on pendentives of the domed ceiling above the sanctuary, which is painted and gilded with *trompe-l'oeil* trefoiled niches with angels and Apostles, and stars in an aquamarine sky. Angels are also in the

tessellated pavement. The choir stalls are carved with Burges's favourite green parrots.

40
St Patrick, Patrington, Humberside
14th–15th century

TA 315225. Patrington, 14 miles (22.5 km) SE of Kingston upon Hull on A1033, on N side of Humber estuary

[A]

The village name comes from the dedication of its parish church, a glorious example of English Decorated, rebuilt on an amazing scale in a continuous construction programme, c.1310–1420. A cruciform church with aisled nave, transepts with east and west aisles, and long chancel, the total length is almost 55 yds (50 m). The slightly later famous spire rises from an octagonal crown of open panels to soar almost 66 yds (60 m) into the sky. Successive medieval Archbishops of York must be given due credit for their patronage.

Near the north door is a large pier base from the earlier church. The five-bay nave arcades have slender piers, the axial shafts keeled, the capitals richly carved with foliage. The church has an abundance of entertaining carvings, on corbels, on the label-stops of arches, and the springers of the aisle vaulting ribs. A string course runs right round the church at window-sill level, running up around the doors. The contemporary font has on each of its twelve sides a much-crocketed and be-finialled niche filled with foliage. Nearby at the back are some early finialled pews, and an 18th-century altar table.

The Jacobean pulpit dated 1612 stands under the tower, the ceiling of which is on large corbels carved with male and female heads. The vertigo-inviting access to the ringing chamber is on steps corbelled out above the east crossing arch. The transepts have three chapels, each with complete piscina, scalloped bowl in trefoiled niche, and

43

St Patrick, Patrington, south arcade. RCHME

head-stopped label. The Lady Chapel, a canted and vaulted east projection from the south transept, retains its original reredos of three ogee-arched panels, the outer two with ball flower ornament, the central one below a steep canopy between pinnacles, now containing a weathered medieval statue of the Virgin and Child.

Across the aisleless chancel is a screen partly of 1496, the lights with wrought-iron grilles. Very large blue marble grave covers have matrices of two brasses, one for a priest. In the north wall is the superb triple-tiered Easter Sepulchre: at the bottom, three crocketed ogee niches each house a sleeping Roman soldier; a cavity, now an aumbry, represents the tomb, and a relief sculpture shows Christ rising from a chest tomb, flanked by two somewhat startled angels; above is a shelved cinque-cusped ogee canopy with large finials. On the south side the three-seat sedilia has uncusped but otherwise matching ogee canopies; the piscina is similar. The reredos, with fifteen mainly northern saints, was installed in 1936.

41

St Paulinus Roman Catholic Church, Brough Park, N Yorkshire
19th century

SE 215981. 1 mile (1.6 km) SW of Catterick Bridge, just S of A6136

[D]

Many North Yorkshire families kept alive the Roman Catholic tradition after the Reformation, and none more ardently than the Lawsons of Brough. Despite persecution, Mass was celebrated daily in a small second-floor chapel in Brough Hall, then with the advent of partial toleration, an elegant Georgian chapel was built onto the house. The 1829 Catholic Emancipation Act allowed public worship, and almost immediately the family built this large and imposing church in the most publicly accessible part of their park. The building, undergoing restoration at the time of writing, is one of the country's greatest

monuments to Catholicism.

William Lawson used architect Ignatius Bonomi of Durham, but was closely involved in the design himself, and decided on a scholarly copy of the 13th-century private chapel of the Archbishops of York, now York Minster Library. Lawson conducted lengthy correspondence with John Browne, the antiquary studying the early architectural history of the Minster after the 1829 fire. Many details, including fittings and stained glass, were based on those in the contemporary Minster transepts. Such an antiquarian approach to Gothic Revival architecture was most unusual in the 1830s, and particularly so for a Roman Catholic Church.

St Paulinus is a surprisingly large two-storey building, in local sandstone with a tall, steep roof of Welsh slates. A school-room originally occupied most of the ground floor. Entry is at the west end into a spacious vestibule, from which twin staircases converge onto a landing, below a large window of five stepped lancets, at the back of the church proper – a large and lofty space of profound meaning, with an arched roof of carved timbers.

Tripled north and south lancets are internally shafted, the capitals and label-stops carved with foliage. To the north is the family pew, behind a stone screen. Below the five-light lancet east window is the stone altar, with five trefoiled arches which enclose a small sarcophagus containing the bones of St Innocent, presented to William Lawson by Pope Gregory XVI.

The altar, St Paulinus Roman Catholic Church, Brough Park. JH

44

42

St Peter, Barton-upon-Humber, Humberside
10th–11th and 14th–15th century

TA 034220. Barton-upon-Humber, on S side of Humber estuary. Town centre

[A] EH

The large square-plan Anglo-Saxon tower of St Peter's originally stood between west and east annexes, perhaps serving as the nave, with baptistery west and chancel east. It has two 10th-century stages, in rendered rubble with long and short quoins and pilaster strip decoration, with a doorway in each side.

The lowest stage, much taller than the second, has two tiers of blind arcading, round-arched below, triangular above. The north and south doorway jambs align with the pilaster strips, and the imposts are square. The north doorway head is triangular, formed of two large stones, the south round-arched with hood-mould. A two-light round-arched window with turned-baluster shaft interrupts both north and south upper arcades.

Each side of the middle stage has a window of two triangular-headed lights, resting on the string course. A third stage, probably of mid-11th-century date, in dressed limestone, has to north, east and south a taller belfry opening, of two round-arched lights with mid-wall shaft of varying design and cushion capital, and a Decorated west window.

The west and east tower arches are decorated with pilaster strips and hood-moulds, but only on the sides facing the tower interior. The east arch was clearly more important, having double-stepped imposts, and a carving above, perhaps a Crucifixion. Above both arches are doorways originally giving access to first-floor chambers in the annexes.

The narrower west annexe has a blocked west door, two small circular windows, one above the other, a small round-arched window to north and south, and a plain-tile pitched roof. The east annexe was superseded by a large

St Peter, Barton-upon-Humber, tower and western annexe from the south. RCHME

aisled church, the nave with Decorated arcades, and the east windows Perpendicular. There is some early brickwork, and the brick north porch has a tumbled gable.

St Peter's is now a monument, as the parish uses St Mary's, which has work of all periods from Romanesque to Perpendicular.

43

Upper Independent Chapel, Heckmondwike, W Yorkshire
19th century

SE 222237. Heckmondwike, on A652 6 miles (9.6 km) NE of Huddersfield. On High Street

[D]

This grandiose Italianate chapel is a sad shell, abandoned by a diminished congregation who decamped to the Sunday School next door. In soot-blackened ashlar sandstone, its projecting portico of four Corinthian columns has the chapel name in solid *sans serif* capitals on the frieze, and over-tall pediment flanked by asymmetrical octagonal turrets over staircase towers. The coursed-sandstone chapel body behind has two storeys of windows reflecting the galleried

interior. The architect was Arthur Alfred Stott, a Heckmondwike man whose sole monument this seems to be.

The historic burial ground dates from the earlier Congregational chapel here. Tombstones include that of the boy-poet Herbert Knowles, whose most famous poem was *The Three Tabernacles or Lines Written in the Churchyard of Richmond, Yorkshire*, of 1816. His antecedents were prosperous Gomersal woollen merchants, but the premature death of both his parents left six young orphans in straitened circumstances. Apprenticed to a London tobacconist, Herbert hated the trade and, feeling a romantic urge to join the army of Wellington, ran away and enlisted. His surprisingly delicate build was later questioned by the regimental chaplain, who discovered his remarkable poetic talent, and arranged for Knowles to receive a belated classical education at Richmond School. There he received the patronage of Poet Laureate Robert Southey, who encouraged Knowles to aim for a place at Cambridge. Struggling to gain the qualifications necessary for university entrance, he succumbed to consumption, and died at Gomersal in 1817 at the age of nineteen.

Upper Independent Chapel, Heckmondwike, south elevation. RCHME

45

44

York Minster, N Yorkshire
12th–15th century

SE 602521. York. In city centre,
N of River Ouse
[A]

The site of the minster recorded by Bede
as newly built in AD 627 has not yet been
found, but carved gravestones suggest
that the pre-Conquest minster was near
the present one. Underneath today's
minster, however, lies Archbishop
Thomas of Bayeux's apsidal-ended late
11th-century cathedral, externally
rendered in a hard white plaster (some
of which may still be seen) on which red
paint lines imitated masonry joints. In
1137 a major York fire caused severe
damage, and *c*.1160 Archbishop Roger
de Pont L'Évêque began a new aisled
square-ended choir above a crypt, the
squat Romanesque columns of which,
refined versions of earlier ones at
Durham Cathedral, exhibit beautiful
workmanship.

The oldest above-ground parts are
the transepts, added *c*.1220–55 to a
much lower Romanesque church by
Archbishop Walter de Gray. His vast
north transept lancets, the Five Sisters,
miraculously retain original grisaille
glass of *c*.1250, its austere greyness and
simple patterning reflecting Cistercian
religious influence. Medieval lead,
buried at Cistercian Rievaulx (25, NY) at
the Reformation, was appropriately used
to repair this window in 1923–5. In the
gentle light of his wheel window in the
south transept stands Walter de Gray's
tomb of *c*.1255, a splendid gabled
canopy on slender shafts, the
composition still Early English, the
ornament almost Decorated.

Later in the 13th century followed
England's largest chapter house, its
Geometric windows almost filling the
eight sides. The intended stone vault
proved too difficult, so it is of wood, as
elsewhere here. The delightful stall
canopies have foliage pendants and
finials, and whimsical head stops. A
model illustrates the forest-like
structure of the pyramidal roof. Above
the L-shaped vestibule from the north

York Minster, the huge nave looking east. ES

transept is a room, with scissor-truss roof, once used as a stone-masons' design office.

Next came the nave, begun 1291 but because of its enormous size a long time in construction. Its design revolutionarily combined triforium and clerestory. Early 14th-century glass in the aisle windows includes a Tree of Jesse on the south side, and on the north one bordered by bells, given by a bell-founder, and its neighbour depicting, along the bottom edge, a funeral procession of monkeys. The large west window was not completed until c.1335, hence its swirling Curvilinear tracery.

That York's is the country's largest cathedral by volume is partly due to the east arm being almost as long as the nave. The Lady Chapel, begun by Archbishop Thoresby in 1360, was built entirely beyond Archbishop Roger's choir, which was then with difficulty replaced. At the junction are quasi-transepts, projecting upward but not outward, thus appearing in elevation but not plan. The great east window, larger than a tennis court in area, was glazed in 1405–8 by an outsider, John Thornton of Coventry. Scenes from the books of Genesis and Revelation can be enjoyed by visitors who bring binoculars.

As work on the Perpendicular choir approached the Early English crossing tower c.1400, the two were out of scale. While attempting to enlarge the tower arches, the masons encountered structural problems, and in 1407 the tower partly collapsed. Deep choir screens were added as strengthening, and a lantern tower built instead of a belfry. The west towers were heightened for bells in the mid–late 15th century. The central tower again gave anxiety and had new foundations inserted in 1967–72. The lack of stone vaults has resulted in an exceptional number of major fires, including two in the 19th century, one in 1829 started deliberately by religious fanatic Jonathan Martin, another in 1840 caused by a careless workman. As recently as 1984 the south transept roof was completely burnt out one summer's night. The ancient stained glass has proved itself remarkably fire-resilient.

York has many fine churches, several with medieval glass: just two are highlighted here. Hidden away in Goodramgate about 330 yds (300 m) south of the minster, Holy Trinity, York's only church to escape Victorian refitting, retains box-pews facing this way and that, leaning drunkenly, providing a catalogue of 17th- and 18th-century hinges and catches. The centre-piece is the now tester-less tall pulpit and reading desk commissioned in 1785. Now vested in the Redundant Churches Fund, the church has early 18th-century chancel fittings, the balustered communion rail of 1715 with central semicircular bow especially notable.

John Walker, who glazed the east window, was rector in 1471–81, making this later than most York stained glass. The figures in this window have autobiographical significance. Walker's membership of the exclusive Corpus Christi Guild is represented in the centre light, with God the Father holding God the Son beside the rector's small red kneeling figure. His membership of the Guild of Sts George and Christopher is illustrated by St George with head painted on an unusually large piece of medieval glass, and a superbly gory dragon, in the first light, and by St Christopher in fish-infested waters in the fifth. Walker's namesakes – St John the Baptist wearing a camel skin still with its head, and St John the Evangelist holding a chalice with dragon emerging from its bowl – are shown in the second and fourth lights respectively.

A chantry chapel was added c.1400 to the south aisle by the Howme family, who sensibly recycled two displaced south-aisle flat-headed and reticulated windows of c.1340. The springers of the wide arch to the chapel are carved with shields 'hung' on hooks by straps: a squint observes the main altar. South of the churchyard Lady Row, York's oldest surviving timber-framing, a jettied terrace of tenements, endowed the church's chantry of the Blessed Virgin. One entrance to the churchyard is from Low Petergate, down Hornpot Lane, where archaeology has shown that medieval craftsmen prepared sheep and cattle horns for a variety of domestic uses, including window panes, lanterns, drinking flasks, combs and hornbooks.

Such a book appears in All Saints, in North Street on the south bank of the River Ouse, a church with many medieval windows of unusual subjects. In the east window St Anne teaches her daughter Mary to read. The south aisle central window, a restored Nine Orders of Angels, has an unexpected delight in a man wearing c.1420 spectacles. The Corporal Acts of Mercy window by John Thornton in the north aisle has a bearded benefactor dispensing charity in everyday contexts, including a medieval sick-room, with bed and commode.

More fearsome is the nearby Last Fifteen Days of the World from a 14th-century northern poem 'The Pricke of Conscience'. The story zigzags up the panel tiers from bottom left: in a 7th-day earthquake a church, like All Saints with slender 15th-century spire, crashes to the ground; on the 13th day, beautiful stars fall to the ground; in the tracery St Peter with keys welcomes good souls to Heaven, a gruesome devil receives the damned.

On the south wall is a monument to John Etty (died 1708), the York carpenter-architect who tutored Grinling Gibbons. Musical angels are carved on 15th-century hammer-beam roofs, those in the chancel repainted in gaudy fairground colours. Equally medieval in character are the chancel screens of 1906 by Edwin Ridsdale Tate, who also did the timber-framed and shuttered-concrete anchorite's cell, with high-level peep-hole into the west end of the church.

4

Castles and Fortifications

The castles included in this chapter were all structures of high social status, indeed several had associations with members of various royal families. Most were bases for the administration of extensive areas as much as they were residences, and all were designed primarily for defence rather than comfortable living, with carefully planned perimeter defences.

The region possesses good examples of a range of castle types. As a general rule, earthwork castles and fortifications, often associated with timber structures, predate those built in stone. The typical early medieval castle consisted of a man-made mound or motte with a defended natural-level bailey. There are fine mottes at **Pickering** (50, NY), **Skipsea** (54, H) and two at **York** (45, NY), also one near **Middleham** (49, NY) at William's Hill. **Helmsley** (47, NY) has an impressive rampart and double ditches.

Many of those early castles were built to express the new regime of the Normans. That at **Richmond** (51, NY) was for this purpose also, but most unusually was of stone from the 11th century and, as a consequence of so early a date for defensive stonework, it exhibits the rare phenomenon of herring-bone masonry in a non-ecclesiastical context. Richmond Castle took such an atypical form for two reasons: its site was naturally superbly suited for defence, and also it was the highly prestigious headquarters of the large area forming the Honour of Richmond.

The disadvantage of earthwork castles was that their buildings were usually of wood, especially on the motte, though Pickering had stone structures in the bailey. Timber structures were vulnerable to attack, and were probably regarded simply as inferior to stone. Large, well-constructed stone keeps afforded more secure, larger and more comfortable accommodation but had to be built directly on the ground, as

artificial mottes could not bear their weight, hence the change of site at Middleham.

Several of the region's mighty 12th-century stone keeps are splendid examples of Romanesque architecture, with regularly sized and shaped ashlar masonry walls rising from battered bases (for deflecting missiles) and with pilaster buttresses articulating their proportions. These walls were so thick that they could accommodate circulation spaces and small chambers. The keep at Richmond, which is rectangular in plan, appears tall and elegant, towering above the older walls below; that at Middleham is extremely large in plan area, and must have looked squat and firm before it was surrounded by curtain walls. The keep at **Scarborough** (53, NY) was another impressive example, but sadly was partially destroyed during the Civil War – its ruined shape was perceived by the author, as a child playing on the sands of the resort's North Bay, as looking like an armchair.

An outstandingly pleasing, if somewhat impractical design was achieved by the designer of the ingenious circular keep at **Conisbrough** (46, SY), which is in a category of architectural excellence on its own. Castle building of the later medieval centuries suggests an increasing appreciation of aesthetics. In the 13th century a more formidable appearance for earthwork castles was achieved by constructing lightweight shell keeps on the mottes. These were not as strong as they looked, but part of one survives at Pickering (50, NY), and York's Clifford's Tower (45, NY) is almost complete. Shell keeps seem to have been a fairly short-lived fashion, and the 14th century saw a return to tower keeps, but these were more elegant in both proportion and detailing than most of their predecessors. Examples include those at Helmsley (47, NY) and **Knaresborough** (48, NY).

Richmond Castle keep, adjacent curtain wall and detention cells. EH

Less survives of the castle at Knaresborough than of most in this chapter, but it is included here for its ingenious sallyport, only recently opened to the public. Sallyports were one of a number of features which reflected developments in military techniques, others being taller gatehouses to receive retracted portcullises, round towers which superseded square ones, thereby avoiding corners which could be undermined, loop-holes which were suitable for cross-bows as well as long-bows, and barbicans providing an outer defence to entrances.

Castles provide some of the earliest evidence of prestigious domestic architecture, and the selection here includes the very early first-floor great hall in the main court at Richmond, and a Romanesque block with fine Elizabethan interior fittings at Helmsley. The region's history of troubled times continuing throughout the medieval period is reflected in its significant numbers of fortified houses, which were not castles as such, and these are here afforded a separate section (chapter 5).

Town defences broadly followed the same historical development as that of castles, with earthworks generally being of earlier date. In only a few places were these replaced in stone, as at York, where the city walls (45, NY) are probably the most famous in the land, because of both their near-complete survival, and also public accessibility. Richmond was enclosed by a wall built because of early 14th-century Scottish incursions, and two postern gates survive (51, NY).

Both Scarborough (53, NY) and Beverley (80, H) towns had defensive ditches, and at the latter the North Bar not only survives but is particularly interesting for its brick building material. Hull (87, H) had walls, of brick, but these have disappeared. At York and Hull the defences were put to exceptionally late use during the Civil War. Defences were constructed against attack from various quarters, including the sea, as at **Hartlepool** (52, C), where the medieval fortifications which protect against the ocean itself, as well as any

threat it might bring, are a particular joy.

Monastic establishments were usually surrounded by a strong perimeter wall, which was occasionally fortified. At York, where St Mary's Abbey occupied a site immediately contiguous to the city walls, as a result of friction between the abbey and the citizens, the abbey built a defensive wall in the 13th century, and as a result of early 14th-century Scottish raids it was crenellated. Much of this wall survives, and the wooden shutters which would have protected the defenders have been restored to the embrasures in a stretch of wall in Marygate.

45

Clifford's Tower and Medieval City Walls, York, N Yorkshire
11th–17th century

Clifford's Tower: SE 605515. Clifford St, York city centre

[A] Clifford's Tower EH

William the Conqueror built two motte-and-bailey castles in York in 1068, one on each bank of the River Ouse. Both were destroyed by the Danes in September 1089, and immediately refurbished. The south motte, known as the Old Baile, survives little changed, measuring 180 ft (55 m) in diameter, 40 ft (12 m) high and 70 ft (21 m) across at the top. The later city wall roughly follows the line of the south-east and south-west ramparts of its rectangular bailey, west of the motte.

The north castle was again rebuilt in timber after destruction by fire during riots of 1190, when Jews taking refuge there were massacred. Clifford's Tower, a quadrilobate shell keep of magnesian limestone was built on the motte at the behest of Henry III, who visited York in 1244. The lower storey had a central pier supporting the floor above, light slits in each lobe, plus a fireplace and garderobe in the two north lobes and staircases to the upper storey in the south lobes. From the upper storey to the west, north and east project inter-lobe bartizans containing a garderobe and staircases to the parapets.

Clifford's Tower, York, from the south-east. EH

The gateway on the south side, with first-floor chapel, was rebuilt when the castle was restored in 1642 by Henry Clifford, 5th Earl of Cumberland, in readiness for a Parliamentarian siege of the Royalist city, and bears his coat of arms below those of Charles I. The Clifford family, hereditary constables of the castle, gave it their name, which was in use by 1600.

The bailey to the south-east, defended by damming the River Foss, was enclosed by a stone curtain wall with round towers by Henry III. After the Civil War the castle remained a prison and court, for which three elegant blocks were built in the bailey. The Vanbrughian Debtors' Prison of 1701 is probably by William Wakefield, the symmetrically classical Assize Courts of 1773 and Female Prison of 1780 are by John Carr. Extensive Tudor-Gothic prison buildings and a perimeter wall of 1825 by P F Robinson and G T Andrews were demolished in 1935.

The castle formed part of York's medieval city defences, which enclosed an area about five times the size of the Roman legionary fortress (13, NY) in its north corner, where the medieval defences overlie the fortress walls. The Norman defences consisted of a rampart and ditch with low stone gateways, known as bars. In the 13th and 14th centuries stone walls were added, and the bars heightened to take portcullises.

The circuit was completed by chains across the River Ouse at Skeldergate and Lendal, and to the east the River Foss was again dammed, to serve also as a fishpond.

Four main gates, three posterns, thirty-nine towers and almost 2 miles (3.2 km) of walls survive. Early 19th-century demolition proposals provoked a conservation protest, and they were eventually reprieved as footpaths, which is why they can be enjoyed as such today. This description of the walls begins north of the erstwhile fishpond at Layerthorpe Postern, passes the fortress east corner tower (13, NY) and leads to the early 14th-century Monk Bar. The only one with a medieval internal elevation, it has vaulted first and second floors as well as carriageway, parapets bearing sculptures of defenders hurling stones, and contains a portcullis with raising mechanism.

The wall to the north-west, which overlies the Roman fortress wall, is notable for exceptional views of the Minster and its Close, and for the clear profile of the ditch outside the rampart in Lord Mayor's Walk. A Roman gateway lies below Bootham Bar, the outer arch of which is that of the squat 11th-century gateway. The 19th-century restorers of the inner facade erred in incorporating loop-holes for attacking the inhabitants!

A demolished stretch of wall necessitates descent here, but crossing St Leonard's to the lane alongside the King's Manor, once the abbot of St Mary's house, finds the medieval wall beside the Multangular Tower (13, NY). This next section can be followed on the ground to the Ouse, where Lendal Tower housed 17th-century pumping mechanisms for the city's water supply.

Across Lendal Bridge the wall can be remounted at North Street Postern, a 14th-century round tower on the river edge. This stretch was breached by the railway for access to the first passenger station inside the walls. By tradition York's Lord Mayor greets the monarch at Micklegate Bar, which faces the London road, and it bears a medieval royal coat of arms, among others. Here heads of traitors were displayed, as Shakespeare observed in *Henry VI*. Its inner face is a more scholarly 19th-century reconstruction.

The wall east of Micklegate was pierced in 1838 for Victoria Bar to give access to a new suburb. The wall near Skeldergate Postern provides a good view of the Old Baile. Cross Skeldergate Bridge, pass York Castle, then Fishergate Postern gives access to the east stretch of wall, only added after 1345. Walmgate Bar, the only one still with a barbican, the outer defence which explains the small doors at a strange level on Monk and Micklegate Bars, also retains its portcullis and 15th-century inner doors, and has an Elizabethan timber-framed inner building. The square Red Tower, built in 1490 in brick, hence the name, marks the start of the fishpond.

46
Conisbrough Castle, S Yorkshire
12th–13th century

SK 515989. Conisbrough, on A630 Doncaster–Rotherham road

[A] EH

Dominating the site, both physically and in exceptionally high quality design and construction, is the splendid keep erected towards the end of the 12th century by Hamelin Plantagenet, 5th Earl Warren. This outstanding example of military architecture is circular in plan, with a battered plinth connected ingeniously to six deeply projecting canted buttresses.

The 15 ft (4.6 m) thick ashlar magnesian limestone wall contains circulation spaces, but was almost impossible to breach with windows, so the interior, though safe from attack, when roofed and floored must have been very dark. It may soon have to be reroofed to halt damage caused by airborne pollution soaking into the stonework with rain.

Steep modern steps replacing the original staircase and drawbridge lead to the first-floor entrance. The doorway has, below a segmental relieving arch of even voussoirs, a flat arch of joggled voussoirs, a feature of the building. A round-arched tunnel through the wall thickness leads to the ashlar-surfaced interior. The ground-floor chamber below is not open to the public, its only access being a central eye in its vaulted ceiling, through which water was drawn from a well.

A gently curving mural staircase rises to the second-floor principal chamber, where a large fireplace hood has a joggled lintel above triple-shafted colonnettes with weathered water-leaf capitals. To its right is a wash-basin, and opposite it, above the entrance, the only window, in a round-arched tunnel vault. Each floor also has a slop-sink.

Another curving, well-lit staircase leads to the lord's private third-floor suite, with smaller similar fireplace above the other, trefoil-headed wash-basin, and a passage to a very good garderobe. A doorway opposite the fireplace leads to the lord's beautiful private oratory, also in the wall thickness, with one round-arched shafted window, two circular windows, and two trefoil-headed piscinas. Two bays of rib vaulting, with decorative bosses, are separated by a chevroned arch. The adjacent vestry, in a buttress, has a trefoiled aumbry.

Conisbrough Castle, third-floor fireplace. RCHME

A final mural staircase leads to the wall-walk around the keep top. The buttress heads are put to good use, one having a guard chamber, another an oven, a third perhaps even a dovecote. There is a good view down into the semicircular inner bailey, surrounded by its curtain wall with solid projecting round towers. A building next to the gatehouse has a complete stone latrine seat – high-grade medieval establishments having almost as many conveniences as a modern multi-bathroomed house!

Instead of the once-ubiquitous wooden hut, in the outer bailey is a modern Visitor Centre, imaginatively designed like a medieval tent. This contains interesting exhibitions, of schoolchildren's work, of medieval life, the Civil War, local industries, and on the *Ivanhoe* connection, for Conisbrough Castle was the inspiration for 'Rotherwood' in Sir Walter Scott's novel.

47

Helmsley Castle, N Yorkshire
12th–14th and 16th century

SE 611836. Helmsley, on A170 Thirsk–Pickering road

[A] EH

The large earthworks, a conspicuous feature of the site, two great rock-cut ditches flanking a steep rampart, were formed by courtier, lawyer and soldier Walter Espec in the 1120s. The quadrilateral area enclosed was further defended by a wall built 1190–1200 by Robert de Roos I. It has round corner towers, except at the south-eastern angle where the main entrance lies, and large towers on the east and west sides.

In the mid-13th century Robert de Roos III added barbicans to the north and south ends of the rampart. The early domestic ranges along the west side were extended into the south-western angle in the early 14th century by William de Roos. The living accommodation was considerably improved by Edward Manners, 3rd Earl of Rutland, in 1563–87. The castle was only abandoned when Duncombe Park

(68, NY) was built early in the 18th century.

Visitors turn left from the present entrance towards the south barbican. The outer gatehouse has round towers, one with garderobe turret. Flanking curtain walls terminate in similar towers. The barbican was enclosed by later walls across the inner ditch, with pointed-arched openings at the bottom. Manners altered the outer front of the gatehouse, but behind is medieval vaulting resting on a Lombard frieze, and a portcullis slot.

The D-shaped east tower, originally only of two storeys, was raised in the 14th century to a four-storey keep with corner turrets, the change in masonry being visible in the west wall, inside which is the scar of the lower pitched roof much below the corbel table of the later roof. The later windows have rib-vaulted heads. A central pier carried basement vaulting, and there was a spiral staircase in the north-west corner. Blown up during the Civil War, the tower's outer half lies in the ditch.

Disguised within the west range is the late 12th-century first-floor hall, part of its round-arched undercroft doorway being visible next to a Tudor doorway below the outside staircase. At the south end of the range, the west solar tower has a 12th-century basement with four large semicircular chamfered ribs, but was rebuilt above in the early 14th century with shouldered doorways, and four storeys of fireplaces on two walls.

The north end of the west range was remodelled in the late 16th century and many fine Elizabethan interior features remain. The large mullion-and-transom windows necessitated many fireplaces: one on the ground floor is very large and four-centre arched; another on the first floor triangular-headed with rolled-and-stopped chamfer. The fine overmantel, dated 1582, has marquetry partly of *trompe-l'oeil* design.

A nearby screen has two tiers of panelling, both with depressed arched heads, and fluted frieze. The plaster frieze above, moulded with sea creatures including mermaids, also has the Rutland arms, still partly painted in heraldic colours. Knots and roses adorn geometrical panels of the rib ceiling.

Another first-floor room has parts of a plaster frieze, and two different Tudor fireplaces.

48

Knaresborough Castle, N Yorkshire
14th century

SE 348569. Knaresborough, 3 miles (4.8 km) NE of Harrogate on A6055

[A]

Philippa, queen to Edward III, received the Honour of Knaresborough in her marriage settlement, and often summered in the royal castle, newly built *c*.1310–40, on a steep cliff above the Nidd gorge. After the Battle of Marston Moor in 1644 the Parliamentarians besieged and captured this Royalist stronghold and rendered it uninhabitable, but the keep was retained as a prison. Its setting is now that of a municipal park, with putting and bowling greens.

Two wards within the curtain wall were separated by a wall, against which the court-house was built in the inner ward opposite the keep. Of the gatehouse in the outer ward, only two solid half-round towers, which flanked the archway, remain. From the outer ward two sallyports led out beyond the curtain wall.

The keep's unusual six-sided plan – square to the inner ward, canted to the gorge – caused problems in vault design. A central pier in the basement supports twelve ribs; the ground-floor chamber has star-like ribs on two piers, and contains an unsorted jumble of archaeological artefacts – lead pipes, stone cannon balls, medieval inscriptions. A small room off has a pointed barrel vault, and an iron window-frame for small geometric panes. A spiral staircase with integral handrail led to the first floor, which had two fireplaces and a wall bench in a large pointed arch.

Mysterious steps in the putting green lead down into the sallyport which has been opened to the public. Tunnelled for 77 yds (70 m) through magnesian limestone, it drops 82 ft (25 m) and

Helmsley Castle, exterior of Elizabethan range. Watercolour by John Hutchinson.

emerges into the dry moat near the gatehouse. A section of the sallyport is grooved as if for a portcullis, though into what this could be raised is unknown. It accommodated only foot soldiers, but the other one was large enough to take ridden horses.

The court-house of *c*.1600 above a 14th-century undercroft contains 17th-century manorial court furnishings. Its museum has displays on eccentric

hermit St Robert, who befriended outlaws, 18th-century road engineer Blind Jack Metcalfe, and Ursula Southeil, better known as 'Mother Shipton'. The over-publicised cave of this semi-legendary prophesying lady is near the more interesting petrifying 'Dropping Well', a curiosity since Elizabethan times, and to which a wooded walk was laid out in the 1740s by the Slingsby family, whose fine monuments are in the parish church.

Knaresborough Castle keep from the east. JH

49

Middleham Castle, N Yorkshire
12th–15th century

SE 128877. Middleham, 1½ miles (2.4 km) SE of Leyburn on A6108

[A] EH

The Honour of Middleham was granted by William the Conqueror to Alan of Brittany, who handed it to his brother Ribald, who in 1086 built a motte-and-bailey castle on William's Hill, an elevated site guarding Coverdale. A century later his grandson, Robert FitzRanulph, built a stone castle ¼ mile away to the north-east on a less

defensive site able to support a substantial structure. Middleham passed by marriage to the Nevilles of Raby, and for part of the 15th century after Anne Neville married the Duke of Gloucester, later Richard III, Middleham played a part in the government of northern England.

The Nevilles improved FitzRanulph's castle over two centuries. Around the square stone keep was added a curtain wall, with square internal corner towers, except for that to the south-west which is round, hollow and projects. Centrally from each side a garderobe tower projects out into the surrounding ditch. The gatehouse in the north-east corner was imposingly rebuilt late in the 14th century. A late 13th-century chapel extended the keep to the east, but service ranges were added to the other three sides of the curtain in the 14th and 15th centuries. For all periods there is a marked visual contrast between the worked brown sandstone used for openings, and grey rubble limestone walling.

Visitors see first the north curtain wall, its pattern of 'put-log' holes indicating the position of medieval scaffolding. The garderobe tower has latrine chutes at the base: inside it can be seen that the facilities were thoughtfully planned to provide access at various levels. The impressive gatehouse, projecting for a drawbridge, has corner buttresses turned diagonally to support bartizans, between which corbels show it had machicolations. The moulded round archway, set within a continuously moulded pointed arch, leads to a tunnel-vault separated by a lateral arch from a rib-vaulted bay, with a portcullis slot at the inside end.

On the east side of the keep the line of the external staircase up to the round-arched first-floor entrance can clearly be seen. The chapel was at that level, so the rooms below it were of lesser significance. Walking round to the south end of the keep demonstrates its size, at 26 yds (23.7 m) by 35 yds (32 m) one of the largest in England, its wall set on a battered plinth. In the centre of the south end, connected by underground drain to the east ditch, is the keep's garderobe tower: this position enabled it

Middleham Castle from the south-west. EH

to serve both main first-floor chambers. The spine wall separating them longitudinally contains the flues of the keep's main fireplaces.

Both first-floor rooms had tall round-arched single-light windows. The Great Chamber to the west was above the kitchen spanned by pointed vaults; the Great Hall to the east was wider, its undercroft requiring parallel barrel vaults supported on five octagonal piers. In the south-east corner a spiral staircase has been restored to allow visitor access to the parapet level, which affords a fine view of William's Hill, as well as of the castle itself, much of Middleham, and a large part of Wensleydale.

50

Pickering Castle, N Yorkshire
11th–15th century

SE 800845. Pickering, on A170 16½ miles (26.5 km) W of Scarborough

[A] EH

The nostalgic sound of steam whistles from the North York Moors Railway adds to the enjoyment of this motte-and-bailey castle. The 11th-century motte, almost 43 ft (13 m) high, sharply profiled, encircled by a ditch and with a well at the base, bears the ruins of the

King's Tower, a shell keep of the 1220s. The inner bailey was in plan a right-angled triangle with northern apex, shortest side to the north-east, and hypotenuse bisecting the motte, with connecting ditches. The bailey's wooden palisades were replaced in the late 12th century by stone curtain walls which enclose the bailey and run up the motte. Entry to the Coleman Tower beside the gateway was from the motte.

In the bailey are foundations of two halls, of c.1180 and 1314, also the reconstructed chapel of c.1226 which, usefully if somewhat incongruously, contains park benches. The outer bailey to the south-east, an addition which makes the motte seem central to the castle plan, has a stone curtain wall of 1323–6 which, strangely for the date, has square projecting towers.

Pickering Castle, the motte from the outer bailey. JH

The Mill Tower in the south corner was entered from the outer bailey by a pointed-arched rib-vaulted tunnel, with a shoulder-headed light vent and a door at each end, like an ice-house. Up the corner stair turret and through a square-headed doorway, the first-floor room has a small square fireplace, garderobe, and pointed-arched window with rib-vaulted head looking to the south.

The 15th-century gatehouse is less impressive than many. To its east the three-storey Diate Hill Tower, entered by a round-arched doorway, has walkway doors with round-arched rib-vaulted heads. To the north-east is Rosamund's Tower, with a basement postern gate to the inner-bailey ditch.

A flavour of the castle's chivalrous past is captured by somewhat over-restored medieval wall paintings in the parish Church of St Peter and St Paul. Above the mid-12th-century north arcade, still with cushion capitals, St George slays a dragon which has apparently rolled over to have its tummy tickled, and a giant St Christopher dis-regards sea-monsters in water around his feet as he bears the Christ-child aloft. Further along St Edmund the King meets his painful bows-and-arrows death. Smaller scenes show Herod's Feast, Coronation of the Virgin and Martyrdom of St Thomas à Becket. Above the late 12th-century south arcade, shafted now with water-leaf capitals, up to four tiers of small scenes include St Catherine's life, Seven Acts of Mercy, Annunciation, Passion, Burial of the Virgin, Resurrection, and a Descent into Hell with ferocious mouth in the arcade spandrel.

The chancel has a Decorated sedilia with crocketed canopies and heads, wall monuments to several aldermen of York, alabaster effigies of a knight and his lady, and a sandstone knight holding his heart in his hands. A north-aisle wall monument commemorates distinguished agriculturalists John and William Marshall, died 1811 and 1818. The church, so thoroughly embattled that even the porch is crenellated, is set high between a network of paths crossing through a crowded churchyard, and the tall west spire is a landmark over the attractive town of Pickering.

51
Richmond Castle, N Yorkshire
11th–15th century

NZ 174006. Richmond, 4 miles (6.4 km) SW of Scotch Corner on A6108 and 3 miles (4.8 km) W of A1

[A] EH

Richmond Castle from the south. EH

Richmond claims the oldest stone-built castle in England, of 1071 and without a timber phase first. Alan of Brittany, granted the Honour of Richmond by William the Conqueror, created an impressive statement of authority on a superb defensive cliff above the River Swale, then apparently a virgin site.

Alan's castle consisted of a large court, triangular in plan with north apex and a base parallel to the Swale. The surrounding stone curtain wall is laid partly in the old-fashioned herring-bone manner of Anglo-Saxon, rather than Norman, architecture. Three square towers projected from the east side, the west angle having a smaller one. There were gates in the south-east corner, the east curtain, and the north apex, the last protected by a barbican and large outer bailey, the first by a small court known as the Cockpit.

In the south-east corner the great hall, named after Scolland, the earl's steward, is a very early example of Norman domestic architecture. Set above an undercroft containing the Cockpit gate, an external staircase led to the large round-arched door of the first-floor hall. This was light and airy, having round-arched windows of two lights, and probably chilly, as they were shuttered but not glazed. The roof sat on a table of corbels carved with masks, spanned by stones shaped into round arcading. At the east end of the hall the earl's more comfortable private solar had a fireplace, and easy access to latrines in the south-east curtain wall tower.

The middle tower has fallen, but that furthest north contains the original castle chapel, dedicated to St Nicholas. Tiny in size, it has built-in wall seats with canopies like the corbel arcading in Scolland's Hall. The Great Chapel in the west corner was founded in 1275, as a chantry served by six canons from Egglestone Abbey in Teesdale. A sallyport gate below it gave access down to the bridge across the River Swale.

About a century after Alan's time, a keep was begun over the north gate by Conan, Duke of Brittany, and completed in the 1180s by that builder of fine military architecture Henry II, guardian to Conan's daughter Constance. The keep is monumental in design, rectangular in plan, and over 100 ft (30 m) high, enabling it to be seen from many vantage points. Its entrance was on the first floor, where there was a main hall, with a staircase in the wall thickness up to the great chamber above, and another up to the parapets.

The 11th-century gateway arch can be seen below the keep. A well, which allowed water to be drawn up to the upper floors, is concealed within a stout pier in the ground-floor chamber. The vault it carries bears the marks of the 14th-century masons who shaped the ribs.

Next to the keep is the 12th-century entrance, alongside which is a block of detention cells built when the castle was the headquarters of the North York Militia. During the First World War the cells housed conscientious objectors to military service, who have left pacifist graffiti pencilled on the plaster walls. In 1855 a now-demolished Tudor-style barrack block was built on the west side of the court. To it in 1908 Lord Robert Baden-Powell, founder of the Scout movement, was sent to plan the layout of a new military camp, which became Catterick Garrison.

52
Sandwell Gate, Hartlepool, Cleveland
14th century

NZ 526335. Hartlepool, 9 miles (14.4 km) N of Middlesbrough on A689. On the Headland

[A]

Hartlepool developed as the major port on the north-east coast due to the early medieval patronage of the de Brus family who, after seizing the Scottish throne in 1306, had to forfeit their English property. In addition to serving the peacetime trade of much of County Durham, Hartlepool was also a convenient port from which to supply the English army during the campaigns of the first three King Edwards against Scotland. On these two counts the port was thus a major target for Scottish raids.

In 1315 the town began to construct defences, initially an earthwork bank

Sandwell Gate. JH

and ditch, improved in the second quarter of the 14th century by the addition of a stone wall. The medieval harbour was a west-facing inlet. To the south, a shore defence was needed against the sea as much as enemies. A considerable stretch survives of this southern defensive wall. Later in the 14th century a gateway was inserted in it.

The Sandwell Gate consists of a single arch, double-chamfered and pointed but with almost straight arcs. It is rebated behind for stout doors, and the wall continues across it on two chamfered ribs. Flanking the arch on the seaward side are large triangular projections, which act as cut-waters as well as protecting the opening.

53

Scarborough Castle and Roman Signal Station, N Yorkshire
Castle: 12th–14th century
Signal Station: 4th century

TA 050893. Scarborough

[A] EH

The natural defence of this precipitous headland has been appreciated since at least the 6th century BC, and a Bronze Age sword was found in 1984. The Romans built here one of a chain of five identical signal stations, part of a coastal defence system of AD *c*.370 against barbarian invasions, using other promontories at Saltburn, Goldsborough and Ravenscar to the north, and Filey further south. The Roman building materials seem to have been incorporated into a Saxon monastery *c*.1000.

An unauthorised castle was built here *c*.1138 by William le Gros – see Skipsea Castle (54, H) – a lawless baron quashed on the accession in 1154 of Henry II, who built a fine tower keep, and retained Scarborough as a royal castle. This provides documentary records of dates and costs: construction took a decade from 1158 and cost £650. The outer bailey south-west curtain wall was gradually built in stone with round

towers, and the main gateway rebuilt 1243–5 by Henry III, its barbican being strengthened *c*.1350.

Minor medieval episodes were eclipsed by sieges of 1645 and 1648 during the English Civil War, both eventually resulting in Royalist surrender, and the keep west wall collapsed after heavy Parliamentarian bombardment in 1645. The castle remained in military and penal use, and in 1665 George Fox, founder of the Religious Society of Friends, or Quakers, was imprisoned here. The Jacobite Rebellion prompted the creation of barracks within some medieval buildings in 1746, also the building beside the keep of a new house for the master gunner. The castle was garrisoned again during the Napoleonic Wars, and military use ceased only after damage in December 1914 during the German navy's shelling of Scarborough.

The castle's three areas – chronologically the large outer bailey on the seaward side, inner bailey with keep, and barbican defending the narrow strip providing the only land access – are seen in reverse order. Entry is by the 1243–5 gateway, round towers protecting its double-chamfered segmental arch. From the barbican curtain walls are stunning views of Scarborough's beaches. The ashlar keep, a fine example of Romanesque military architecture, was square in plan, with battered base, corner shafts, pilaster buttresses and round-arched windows. It was entered on the first floor by an external staircase for further security, and an arched spine wall bisected the two top floors. The basement was utilitarian.

Across the ditch and outer bailey is the Roman signal station, partly now lost to the North Sea. A square timber tower, 100 ft (30 m) high, surrounded by a stone wall with corner turrets, stood within a ditch. The nearby Saxon chapel formed from its ruins has within its rebuilt vaulted structure an 18th-

Scarborough Castle, the keep from the south-west. EH

century army brick water-tank, a mix of dates and functions typical of the site. Interpretation is further complicated by works of William le Gros and Tudor occupants. Another bracing walk across springy turf along the cliff edge reaches the south end of the curtain wall, where a medieval sallyport was utilised to provide access to a Civil War battery below. The return journey passes the basement of Mosdale Hall, a medieval domestic range, and the foundations of a large Romanesque great hall.

54

Skipsea Castle, Humberside
11th century

TA 162550. Skipsea Brough, ¼ mile (0.4 km) W of Skipsea and 8 miles (12.8 km) S of Bridlington via A165 and B1242

[A] EH

The lordship of Holderness was granted by William I to Drogo de Bevrere, the husband of a kinswoman. The site and plan chosen for his castle were ingenious, bearing in mind the low-lying nature of the area, then a shallow lake, Skipsea Mere. On an island he constructed a large motte 45 ft (13.8 m) high, its summit ⅕ of an acre (0.08 ha) in extent, to provide plenty of space for wooden buildings to accommodate his household in case of attack. On the east side are remains of a stone wing wall. The motte's surrounding ditch was defended to the north and east by an outer rampart.

To the west and south was a kidney-shaped bailey, again unusually large at 8½ acres (3.4 ha), separated from the motte by the Mere, with an access causeway. Though since drained, visitors will become aware of the part played by water in the site's defences, for the approach is extremely muddy! The Mere also provided a source of eels. Around the outer edge of the bailey, forming a crescent in outline, is a fine rampart and outer ditch, with two gateway openings west and east of its

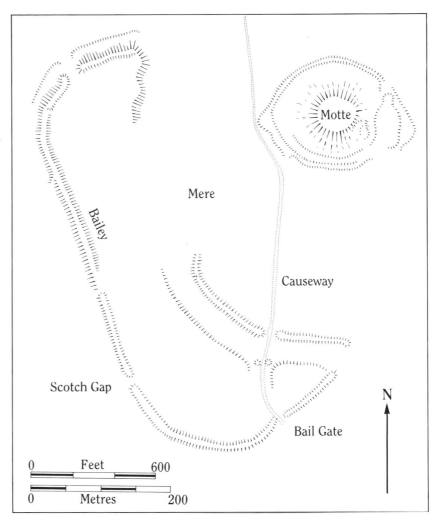

Skipsea Castle. EH

south end.

Drogo soon fell from the Conqueror's favour, for in 1086 he murdered his wife, and his lands were confiscated. The nepotism continued, however, for they were allocated by William Rufus to Odo, Count of Champagne, married to the Conqueror's sister, the Countess of Aumale. Odo too soon transgressed, by taking part in the Mowbray rebellion of 1094 in support of his nephew Stephen against the king, and was imprisoned and his lands forfeited.

The same Stephen received the lands

from Henry I, and although he too dabbled in treason, he kept them and passed them to his son William le Gros, Count of Aumale and Earl of Albemarle. He was a principal commander at the Battle of the Standard, fought near Northallerton in 1138, and was created Earl of York, but was otherwise an aggressive trouble-maker in the area. His son, another William, then abandoned Skipsea in the mid-13th century, and the castle went out of commission, which explains its lack of stone buildings.

5

Fortified Houses

This region includes the southern edge of the area where fortified houses mainly occur. Usually of later medieval date, many were built during the period of Scottish incursions, particularly in the early 14th century. Others are of 15th-century date, and represent unease during the Wars of the Roses. After this period the Tudors' more peaceful times were reflected in domestic architecture taking less account of defence.

It can be difficult to decide whether a building is a fortified house or a castle, and the confusion is compounded by many a fortified house having the word 'castle' in its modern name. The author's definition is that the primary concept of a castle is defence, with accommodation taking second place, whereas the primary purpose of a fortified house is domestic, although it incorporates defensive features. Fortified houses were often built by rather lesser families than those which owned true castles, and some were built by people who were themselves aggressive to their neighbours, and therefore knew they could anticipate counter-assault.

A fortified house rarely has outer defences, though **Markenfield Hall** (57, NY), and **Skipton Castle** (59, NY) do. **Bolton Castle** (55, NY) is on the borderline between castle and fortified house, but its innovative design with central courtyard is of national importance, and looks forward to a period of increasing comfort in great houses. It is one of two houses in this selection which express the holding of high office of state by their builder: the other, Markenfield (57, NY), is very different, though it too gives great pleasure to visit, and is one of few northern examples of a house additionally fortified by a water-filled moat.

Fortification took various forms. Often there was some stone vaulting, for fire-proofing reasons. Usually there was some kind of tower, for look-out as well as ballistic purposes, so the roof was flat (and covered in lead which was mined in the Yorkshire Dales). The roof would have a crenellated parapet, and the staircase up to it a protective turret at the top. Records of licences issued by the Crown for the crenellation of houses are an important source of dating evidence for the near-completion of building works. The tower is the solar block at Markenfield (57, NY) and **Spofforth** (60, NY). Occasionally there were two fortified towers, one at both high and low ends of the great hall, as at Nappa in Wensleydale (NY). Sometimes the house lay on the north side of a courtyard defended by a wall, which at Walburn in Swaledale (NY) has a parapet walk and battlements.

A peel-tower was small in area, and generally originally associated with buildings of less substantial construction. Included in chapter 7 is that at Ripley (91, NY). A tower-house contained all the accommodation within a single tower, usually quite generous in plan area, but lowish in height. Most surviving examples of this category of northern fortified house are private homes without public access. The sole example included here is **Gilling Castle** (56, NY), which is also important for its particularly fine Elizabethan great chamber and early 18th-century additions.

Two of the entries, the **Marmion Tower** (58, NY) and the gatehouse at **Steeton Hall** (61, NY), are solitary gatehouses, without their complementary medieval buildings, but both are fine examples, and the former is associated with particularly interesting medieval funerary monuments.

Marmion Tower from the north. EH

Bolton Castle from the west. Watercolour by John Hutchinson.

55

Bolton Castle, N Yorkshire
14th century

SE 033918. Castle Bolton. On N side of Wensleydale, N of Hawes–Leyburn stretch of A684

[A]

Sited visually to dominate much of Wensleydale, Bolton Castle is among the country's most important 14th-century secular architecture, because although well fortified, it was more comfortable and elegant than earlier castles. The building contract survives for much of the work, between Lord Richard Scrope, Chancellor of England in 1379, the year he was licensed to crenellate, and John Lewyn, a national figure among master masons.

His revolutionary design provided independent apartments and lodgings, of varied size and status, enjoying communal cooking and eating facilities and chapel, but each with its own fire-place and garderobe. The plan, a quad-rangle of ranges facing the cardinal points, permits larger windows onto the central courtyard than would have been wise in the outer walls. Four square corner towers project, taller by two floors than the three-storey side ranges. Garderobe turrets project from the centre of the north and south ranges, which are longer than those to west and east.

The gatehouse just north of the south-east corner tower has a portcullis at each end of its barrel-vault. Doorways into the ranges from the courtyard, each protected by a portcullis on the wall face, are symmetrically arranged, on the north and south sides beside the corner towers, plus another on the east side. Where the corner towers abut the courtyard, they are extended out over it as diagonal turrets, supported on squinches, further to defend the vulnerable corner access points.

The ground floor was mainly service space, living rooms being on first and second floors. The large hall for communal dining and entertaining was two storeys high, in the north range to have sunny windows facing south into the courtyard. The tall single-light windows, with single transom, contained vents in their heads through which smoke escaped from the central hearth. The kitchen, conveniently close in the north-east corner tower, does not survive, having been deliberately demolished to make the castle

uninhabitable when it was surrendered after a lengthy Civil War siege in 1644.

The chapel, on the second floor of the south range, was unusual in having full-size windows in the outside wall. The apartment in the south-west corner, thus closest to the chapel, was the best state suite, and so was assigned to Mary, Queen of Scots during her imprisonment here in 1568. Some of its windows were enlarged, giving splendid views into Wensleydale. The rooms in this corner have particularly grand fireplaces, also ingeniously arranged garderobes, each with a discreet mural passage, slop-basin and small window.

56

Gilling Castle, N Yorkshire
14th, 16th and 18th century

SE 611768. Gilling East, on B1363 Oswaldkirk–Brandsby road

[B]

Now a boys' preparatory school, occupying an elevated site above church and village, Gilling Castle presents marked contrasts: to the east an Elizabethan house, somewhat stark externally but internally sumptuous; to the west an early 18th-century house, also with good interiors – both phases by the recusant Fairfax family who also built the mid-18th-century Fairfax House in York (95, NY). Encased within, however, is part of the Etton family's mid–late 14th-century fortified tower-house, of unusually large size, about 26 yds (24 m) square.

Its ground floor, now the main range basement, has a spine corridor with pointed tunnel vault, off which three pointed-arched doorways in both the north and south flanking walls lead to service chambers. Each end of the corridor has a pointed-arched doorway, that to the east more elaborate and with an outside portcullis slot. In front of this entrance a later staircase tower is externally polygonal. Large Elizabethan mullion-and-transom windows, some in canted bays, are three lights high on the first floor, two on second.

Sir William Fairfax's first-floor great

Gilling Castle from the south-east, in 1908. CL

chamber, now the boys' dining room, is of great importance, not least because it was sold and removed from the house, and has been restored to it. Its heraldic enamelled window glass, signed by Baernard Dinninckhoff, is dated 1585. Three-tier wall panelling, each square with central lozenge, is inlaid with contrasting woods. The Fairfax coat of arms on the richly carved chimney-piece is flanked by shell niches, framed by Corinthian columns, with royal arms above, below a pediment. The chamber's frieze is painted with heraldry of local gentry families depicted in punning manner on trees and, in one corner, the figures of six of the musicians who must have entertained there. The ceiling has a geometric pattern of ribs, formed into pendants.

The west front was added by William Wakefield, a gentleman architect born nearby at Huby and educated at Coxwold Grammar School (82, NY), and is one of his few works attributable with certainty. The principal floor, between high basement and attic storey, has an open staircase leading to a central pedimented door-case, and windows with Gibbs surrounds. The parapet has urns. The flanking projecting wings, longer than the five-bay elevation they

frame, have canted side bays near their outer ends.

The groin-vaulted entrance hall, with elaborate Fairfax coat of arms above the fireplace, has good Italianate plasterwork by Giuseppe Cortese. Corridors leading off are screened by round arches draped with cornucopiae,

on paired Corinthian columns. The staircase has balusters richly carved with an upturned column-on-gadroon-on-bell. Good plasterwork is also in the north wing rooms, where over-door panels have strangely shaped raised centrepieces, and one room has a pretty corner fireplace. Fittings from the south wing long gallery are now in the Bowes Museum at Barnard Castle, County Durham.

57

Markenfield Hall, N Yorkshire
14th and 16th century

SE 294674. W of A61 Ripon–Harrogate road 3 miles (4.8 km) S of Ripon, 1 mile (1.6 km) up a farm track marked only as a footpath to Hellwath

[A] Monday afternoons in the summer season

The access track gives no hint of this Decorated period moated manor house until earthworks appear to the right, then buildings. Farm sheds neatly fit into a symmetrical pair of agricultural ranges, of 17th- and 19th-century date, serving the extra purpose of ensuring a formal approach to the gatehouse from

Markenfield Hall, fireplace in the hall undercroft. RCHME

the south. First stroll to right and left to see the outer elevations of the west and east ranges, and admire black swans and other birds on the moat.

Licence to crenellate was granted in 1310 to Exchequer Chancellor John de Markenfield, who gave architectural expression to that post, perhaps having visited other state officers, for this does not feel like Yorkshire. Queen Elizabeth confiscated the hall from Sir Thomas Markenfield after the Rising of the North and granted it to her Lord Keeper, Sir Thomas Egerton, who made alterations and built the gatehouse. Markenfield was sold to Fletcher Norton, Speaker of the House of Commons and Baron Grantley of Markenfield from 1782, but he moved 4 miles (6.4 km) west to Grantley Hall, since disposed of. Markenfield became and remains a tenanted farm, the glorious buildings amicably shared between the 7th Lord Grantley and his tenants.

The moat encloses a quadrangle with Egerton's gatehouse and flanking stone walls to the south – the original entrance being in the east side, now the farmhouse – and ranges to the west, north and east, with the main buildings forming the north-east corner. To the east is the solar wing, converted from two to three storeys by Egerton, with two-light mullioned windows, its projecting turret housing a spiral staircase up to the roof.

To the north the first-floor hall has tall two-light pointed-arched windows, with roll-moulded mullion and transom and Geometric tracery. Water-tabling marks its doorway, and oblique lines in the cobbles pick out the site of an external staircase. A small window has a leaf carved on its lintel. A kitchen was added to the west early in the 15th century. Visitors enter by a small door into the hall undercroft, the large arched fireplace, inserted in the 18th century, containing a huge kitchen range with oven, water boiler and reckon complete with pot-hooks. The buttress left of the door, once for a garderobe, now appropriately provides a lavatory.

An east door leads to part of the vaulted solar undercroft, its heavy chamfered ribs resting on corbels to the left, and on piers to the right. The west window of the hall, up a 19th-century staircase, was blocked by the later kitchen. A pointed-arched doorway in the south-east corner is to the chapel, with matching three-light east window, aumbry, and a delightful piscina with the Markenfield coat of arms on a once-double basin, the canopy with large crockets and 'stellar' vaulting. The door nearby was a squint to the adjoining chamber, an antique radiator now occupying the original doorway. A gallery across the west end connected sections of the inserted second floor. Niches in the north wall date from recent and tactful strengthening work.

58

Marmion Tower, N Yorkshire
15th century

SE 267787. West Tanfield, on A6108 Masham–Ripon road

[A] EH

Tomb of Sir John and Lady Elizabeth Marmion in St Nicholas Church, West Tanfield. RCHME

The 18th-century bridge across the River Ure gives a splendid view of West Tanfield church and the Marmion Tower beside it, built c.1410 by Sir Henry Fitzhugh. He married Marmion heiress Elizabeth, and their son Robert Fitzhugh was Bishop of London. The tower is not only a fortified gatehouse protecting the Marmions' lost medieval castle, but is in itself a small house of quality. It displays many designs for windows (the grooves for lead cames and the rebates and hinges for shutters can be seen), doorways (some with an adjacent recess for the door to open back into) and fireplaces.

The unbuttressed ashlar sandstone building has a crenellated parapet, to defend the erstwhile flat roof: visitors can climb the spiral staircase to this level. Completely separate from the genteel rooms above is the porter's lodge, with Tudor-arched doorway, small moulded window, large fireplace, garderobe and pointed barrel vault. It is south of the roadway, which has a four-centred arched barrel vault, with head-stopped label to each outer arch. There was no portcullis, but the walls have rebates into which great wooden doors folded back.

Corbelled out from the east side of the first-floor chamber, a beautiful oriel window has panel tracery above cinque-cusped lights. The south wall has a trefoiled window and mural garderobe recess, the west side a mullion-and-transom window, the north side a fireplace. The second-floor fireplace is on the west side, also a pointed mullion-and-transom window with trefoiled top lights. The north wall has a single-light window, the east side a mullion-and-transom window with seats, the south side a trefoiled two-light window in pointed opening and a Tudor-arched doorway to the garderobe, which is corbelled out externally.

The Marmion family lie in the adjacent church of St Nicholas. Along its north wall are several recumbent male and female effigies, mostly of sandstone, but one limestone lady may be Maud Marmion, foundress of mid-14th-century chantries here. Hers was probably the fine *ex situ* Decorated tomb recess, its pointed arch with pierced cusps below a crocketed canopy, between thin fluted pinnacles joined by ball-flower motif. It now contains an earlier 14th-century effigy of a knight in chain mail.

The finest monument is that of Sir John Marmion (died 1387) and his wife Elizabeth St Quintin (died 1400). Their Derbyshire alabaster figures lie on a brattished limestone chest, below a wrought-iron hearse, crenellated and with leaf prickets for candles. He wears plate armour and a Lancastrian collar, his head resting on his plumed tilting helmet, feet on a lion, her head gently held by angels, feet on a lion which retains its very long tail.

Medieval glass in the north chapel's north-east window shows heraldry of the Marmion and related families. A lobby-like structure between the Marmion Chapel and chancel was perhaps for a chantry, a small extension to the south nave wall may be another. In the chancel floor a small brass to rector Thomas Sutton (died 1492) portrays him in Mass vestments, with Latin inscription.

Skipton Castle, Conduit Court. RCHME

59
Skipton Castle, N Yorkshire
13th–17th century

SD 991519. Skipton, 18 miles (28.9 km) NW of Bradford via A650(T) and A629(T)

[A]

The castle, and Tudor east range, sit above a steep drop to the north. The part open to the public, around a small, irregular courtyard, dates from c.1200, with round towers of the early 14th century, when the Clifford family became lords of Skipton. Tudor Cliffords had royal connections, and George Clifford, 3rd Earl of Cumberland, was Queen Elizabeth's Champion. His wife founded Beamsley Hospital (96, NY), and their daughter, Lady Anne Clifford, restored the castle after its Civil War siege.

The detached south gatehouse has round towers flanking a later four-centred arch, with the Clifford arms above, and their motto *DESORMAIS* in the open parapet. Inside is an early shell grotto. Ahead are formidable hollow round towers on battered plinths; to the

right the Tudor range; to the left the derelict chapel with fragmentary Decorated window tracery, sedilia niche, aumbries and king-post roof.

The early Tudor castle entrance, beasts in its doorway spandrels, has an inscription commemorating Lady Anne's restoration, below an oriel window. The original gatehouse round arch, with portcullis groove, leads to the Conduit Court, where water was brought from outside, its ancient yew tree said to have been planted by Lady Anne. Her great-great-grandfather Henry, 10th Lord Clifford, 'The Shepherd' who as a Lancastrian fled to his rural Cumberland estate during Yorkist supremacy in the Wars of the Roses, created the courtyard buildings with windows of round-arched lights without tracery. Lead rain-water heads cast with the date *1659* and initials *AP*, for Anne, Countess of Pembroke, commemorate her reroofing. A bewildering number of doors lead off the courtyard to rooms at many different levels, and the castle is ideal for games of hide-and-seek.

Post-Civil War repair was also needed at the nearby Perpendicular parish church of Holy Trinity, where window quarries show *AP*. In the south chancel is the chest tomb, shields on its black marble slab giving Clifford genealogy, which Anne commissioned for her gallant father in 1654, almost fifty years after his death in London. In the north chancel the tomb of Henry Clifford, 1st Earl and Knight of the Garter, died 1542, and his second wife Margaret Percy, has portrait brasses inset into the polished marble lid, and a vertical panel at the east end with brasses of Henry, 2nd Earl, and his family.

A just-pre-Reformation chancel screen – richly-carved tracery to four-light bays, luxuriantly-twined foliage to top rail – has angels, which once carried the rood loft on inter-bay posts. The late-medieval flat roof is richly moulded, with ties on traceried and cusped brackets, bosses pendant from short central struts. Above the south aisle four-seat sedilia hangs a royal coat of

arms of 1798. Near the south door a medieval wall-painting shows the hand of Death.

60

Spofforth Castle, N Yorkshire
13th–15th century

SE 360511. Spofforth, 3 miles (4.8 km) NW of Wetherby on A661 Wetherby–Harrogate road

[A] EH

A fortified manor house granted to the Percy family, Spofforth Castle's fortunes waxed and waned with theirs, being confiscated, returned, lost, won back, restored, and finally ruined during the Civil War. In pink-brown sandstone quarried on site, the design – L-shaped range originally with courtyard to the east – made ingenious use of the land-

fall to the west, the main rooms being at courtyard level, from which rock-hewn steps lead down to the undercroft.

The early 13th-century hall undercroft, built against the east rock face, has single-light west windows with trefoiled rear arches, and octagonal piers for a vault. External walls have plinths, buttresses to resist vault thrust, and scars from put-log holes of medieval wooden scaffolding. The hall, upgraded in the 15th century, was entered from the courtyard by a porch, through a continuously moulded pointed-arched doorway with hood-mould, its head ribbed inside. Five bays of cusped two-light windows have pointed arches with hood-moulds to the outside, rib-vaulted segmental arches inside.

Henry Percy's licence to crenellate in 1308 related to defensive works then being completed on the north solar wing, where the chapel has a two-light window with Geometric tracery. A spiral

Spofforth Castle from the west. EH

staircase in the north-west corner led up to the roof, where the turret still terminates in a stone conical roof with apex finial. On the ground floor are two pointed-arched hearths, between the springing of vaults which spanned right across the solar undercroft.

61

Steeton Hall Gateway, N Yorkshire
14th century

SE 484314. On minor road ½ mile (0.8 km) W of South Milford, 4 miles (6.4 km) N of Ferrybridge

[A] EH

Of *c*.1360, in ashlar magnesian limestone, looking almost like a folly from the road, this gatehouse has two double-chamfered archways, small and round to left for pedestrians, larger and segmental for vehicles. Above the dividing pier is the corbelled chimney of a first-floor chamber fireplace, and to its left a light slit for the staircase giving it access. At a higher level above the larger arch is a small shoulder-headed watching window. The prominently crenellated parapet projects on corbels carved with heraldic and similar devices. To the left survives a short stretch of battlemented wall.

Steeton Hall gateway, inner side. EH

The archway walls have no portcullis slot, but are rebated for gates, a crook for which remains. The pedestrian opening has a tunnel-vault with chamfered ribs, the carriageway a quadripartite rib-vault. The inside elevation has a pointed-arched doorway to a ground-floor guard-room, and external steps up to an ogee-headed first-floor doorway. A cusped single-light first-floor window has been converted to a pigeon-cote.

Near the gatehouse are disused 18th-century farm buildings. The complex medieval hall itself, not open to the public, is partly derelict and partly Victorianised. On flat farmland nearby, the Battle of Towton was fought in a snowstorm on Palm Sunday 1461, when the Lancastrians lost to the Yorkist army: it is amazing that this gatehouse could have survived that slaughter.

6

Country Houses and Gardens

This chapter covers the provision of superior domestic accommodation of a mainly unfortified kind, and therefore generally follows on from castles (chapter 4) and fortified houses (chapter 5). A chronological exception included here, however, is the Norman manor house at **Burton Agnes** (65, H), which does not present a fortified appearance. However, its main living area is on the first floor, above a vaulted undercroft, and the building may originally have looked more defensive before its elevations were altered.

Undefended medieval houses occur in other chapters, such as Shandy Hall, Coxwold (82, NY), and Shibden Hall, Halifax (84, WY). The medieval tradition survives in a 17th-century house in a relatively remote location, Braithwaite Hall (NT, 3 miles (4.8 km) S of Leyburn in Wensleydale), and in the same area a more vernacular house at Countersett (31, NY) is mentioned in chapter 3.

The region has an important Elizabethan house at Burton Agnes (see 65, H), designed by Robert Smythson, the leading northern architect of his day, and another, also in Humberside, at Burton Constable (8 miles (12.8 km) NE of Hull). Brief descriptions of high quality Elizabethan interiors are to be found in other chapters – the west range of Helmsley Castle (47, NY), and Gilling Castle (56, NY), a fortified house with an extremely fine great chamber of the 1580s.

Several houses are mainly of 17th-century date, and well illustrate the changes in house plan, and materials, which then occurred in the region. **East Riddlesden Hall** (69, WY) and Nunnington Hall (NT), 4½ miles (7.2 km) SE of Helmsley (NY), were both old-fashioned for their time, whereas **Kiplin Hall** (73, NY) and Moulton Hall (NT, 4 miles (6.4 km) NE of Richmond) have compact plans. Kiplin Hall is in brick, as is **Temple Newsam** (79, WY), which still had narrow ranges forming a courtyard. **Newby Hall** (74, NY) and

Castle Howard (66, NY) were both begun in the 1690s, and both were remarkably advanced for Yorkshire design at that time, but the former is almost a typical 'Queen Anne' house, whereas the latter is on an almost unique scale of innovation and grandeur.

Sir John Vanbrugh is not, however, by any means the only famous name to be represented here. In complete contrast to the scale of Castle Howard is Colen Campbell's minute gem, **Ebberston Hall** (70, NY). The major local architect William Wakefield designed **Duncombe Park** (68, NY) and the additions to Gilling Castle (56, NY). The other two major early 18th-century houses in the region were **Bramham Park** (63, WY), designed by its owner, and **Beningbrough Hall** (62, NY) by William Thornton, who for the entrance hall was clearly inspired by Wakefield's groin-vaulted entrance hall at Gilling Castle.

By the mid-18th century the Baroque had given way to Palladianism, as at **Nostell Priory** (75, WY), begun by James Moyser and continued by James Paine, who also completed **Cusworth Hall** (67, SY). John Carr designed **Harewood House** (72, WY), but it was completed by Robert Adam, as were the extensions at Newby Hall. **Ormesby Hall** (76, C) is also of two phases. Wentworth Woodhouse (near Rotherham, SY), which boasts the longest English house elevation, and to parts of which the names of most leading 18th-century architects have at some time been ascribed, is omitted from this selection primarily because it is not open to the public.

Many of the houses in this chapter are an amalgam of several periods of work, but **Brodsworth Hall** (64, SY) is one of the most complete late 19th-century country houses surviving, with art collections of the period. **Sledmere House** (77, H), although apparently Georgian, is largely one of the finest examples of Edwardian workmanship. It was rebuilt after a fire. Many of the

Castle Howard, Great Hall. CL

Nostell Priory, entrance front. NT

62
Beningbrough Hall, N Yorkshire
18th century

SE 517586. Beningbrough, 2 miles (3.2 km) W of A19 York–Thirsk road, 7 miles (11.2 km) NW of York

[A] NT

The National Trust joined forces with the National Portrait Gallery to hang important pictures of the right period in the main rooms of Beningbrough Hall, and a top-floor architectural exhibition

houses contain craftsmanship of particularly excellent quality, notably Harewood House (72, WY), Newby Hall (74, NY) and Nostell Priory (75, WY), which were designed by Robert Adam. Earlier plasterwork of exquisite quality by Giuseppe Cortese survives at Temple Newsam, also at Gilling Castle (56, NY), and at Newburgh Priory (82, NY). More of his work can be seen at Fairfax House in York (see 95, NY), where there is much fine wood-carving. William Thornton, carpenter-architect of Beningbrough Hall (62, NY), also did fine carving at Gilling Castle (56, NY), and some at Ebberston Hall (70, NY).

The region has many good landscaped gardens, including several of early date. Early-18th-century water gardens survive substantially at Bramham Park (63, WY) and Ebberston Hall (70, NY). Templed terraces of two periods survive at and near Duncombe Park. Two of the three remarkable landscapes created by the Aislabie family in Yorkshire are included here: **Studley Royal** (78, NY) and **Hackfall** (71, NY); the other being at Kirkby Fleetham. A fine early example of a Gothick folly at Richmond, Culloden Tower (see 90, NY), is a remnant of a lost 18th-century garden of some importance. 'Capability' Brown landscapes survive at Burton Constable, Harewood House, Sledmere and to some extent at Roche Abbey (26, SY) and Temple Newsam. An early 20th-century garden of great charm can be seen in Richmond at a house called St Nicholas.

Beningbrough Hall, the main staircase. NT

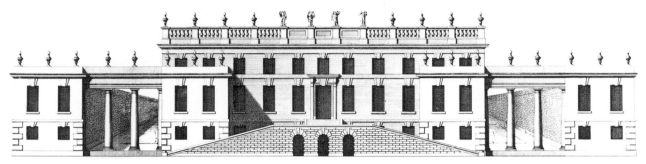

Bramham Park, east elevation from *Vitruvius Britannicus* (vol II, plate 81). RCHME

includes portraits of famous architects. The house, in small orange and red bricks, with ashlar quoin strips and bands, was completed *c*.1716 for John Bourchier. The designer was York carpenter-architect William Thornton, and the details show a wood-carver's hand.

The interior is Baroque, in both decorative style and spatial effects. The outside is plainer: a long, narrow eleven-bay house with two storeys of tall sash windows, those to the attic being squeezed between large paired brackets which, though of stone, look as if they should be carved wood. The south garden front stresses only end bays and a central Ionic door-case with Baroque segmental pediment; the north entrance front stresses three centre bays and two at each end. Here flanking box-like pavilions – bell cupolas ingeniously supported on pendentives over pyramidal roofs – project forward from the house, linked by right-angled single-storey brick walls. Open archways bring visitors through these pavilions from each side, making them turn through a right angle before facing the house.

The square central entrance hall is two storeys high: from a deep dado giant-order Corinthian pilasters reach up, as if only just to touch, the coved ceiling which drops downwards in groined vaults. Doorways and corridor openings are round-arched, and have on the first floor excellent wrought-iron panels, probably by Robert Bakewell.

The house features bolection panelling, projecting deeply into rooms and with richly carved Baroque details wrapping three-dimensionally around the friezes. Doric triglyphs grow up into voluted brackets in the smoking-room frieze, painted a plum colour, but several rooms have pine stripped by the Earl and Countess of Chesterfield in the 1920s, as two small closets seen next, their corner fireplaces ledged to display blue-and-white china.

The south rooms' doors align for an enfilade view along the full house length. A bedchamber – with amazingly tall bed – has a frieze of luxuriant acanthus leaves and masks showing the four seasons, and ornate picture frames carved over fireplace and two doors. The dining room, with less opulent painted panelling, displays portraits of Kit Cat Club members. The Chesterfields combined the best state suite's connecting rooms into a drawing room: the former withdrawing room's exquisite frieze has paired acanthus brackets, the bedchamber's curving plinths between richly carved panels incorporating the initials of John Bourchier and his wife Mary.

Pedimented door surrounds with twisted acanthus buds are seen from the secondary staircase. The large south-facing panelled saloon has coved ceiling, gilded Corinthian pilasters and friezes, and oval-panelled dado. A bedroom has circular medallions within fruit drops to over-door panels, and its closet offers a period bathroom with original carved marble buffet fountain. Balcony views of halls below are afforded by a main axis first-floor corridor: the exquisite main staircase, with panels of delicate woodwork imitating wrought-iron between turned balusters, has wide marquetry treads, and half-landings inlaid with the date *1716* and the Bourchiers' initials.

63

Bramham Park, W Yorkshire
18th century

SE 408417. 1 mile (1.6 km) W of A1, 4 miles (6.4 km) S of Wetherby

[A]

Frosted-rusticated gate-piers by Thomas Archer grace the east front of this soft magnesian limestone house, the central two-storey block, with lower projecting wings, linked by Doric colonnades to pavilions. The west garden front is elegantly simple, only gentle modelling of the end walls and end bays breaking the severity. To the south a dramatic stable block, perhaps by James Paine, has a central portico and cupola, and end pavilions; in its courtyard foxhound puppies play, exotic fowl with chicks like mobile powder-puffs cluck underfoot and peacocks call from rooftop vantage points.

The house is unporticoed due to the early date – finished by 1710 according to Colen Campbell in the second volume of his *Vitruvius Britannicus* (a seminal book of architectural designs), published in 1717. No architect is known; seemingly the designer was Robert Benson himself, later first Lord Bingley, a self-made man, Lord Mayor and Member of Parliament for York. He was a favourite of Queen Anne, and her portrait by Kneller hangs above the bolection-moulded fireplace opposite Reynolds' *Duke of Cumberland* in the two-storey entrance hall. Its ashlar walls have giant Corinthian pilasters and rich cornice, the doors three fielded panels. Other pleasing rooms retain few original features as there was a major fire in 1828, but have the charm of being lived in.

Having made such a good job of designing the house, Lord Bingley then laid out to its west superb French-inspired formal gardens, which survive remarkably intact, and have been very little romanticised. They consist of beech trees (still magnificent despite severe damage during a 1962 gale) forming avenues which provide vistas to temples, statues, an obelisk, water features and the house.

The pleasure grounds are separated from the surrounding park by a retaining wall with projecting bastions. One of these frames one end of the T-shaped canal, hidden from the house by its position on higher ground. A Gothic temple stands above a sloping lawn which sweeps down towards a series of fountains and formal ponds on stepped levels, subtly sited so that from certain positions some are hidden from view. The sunken rose garden outside the west front was once another series of cascades and pond.

64

Brodsworth Hall, S Yorkshire
19th century

SE 500070. Brodsworth, 5 miles (8 km) NW of Doncaster, off B6422

[B] ([A] from 1995) EH

This Italianate mansion, glimpsed across arable fields in a landscape surprisingly unscarred by coal-working, was built for Charles Sabine Thellusson from the proceeds of a will dispute. The case, resolved after sixty years by the House of Lords, formed the model for *Jarndyce v. Jarndyce* in *Bleak House*, Charles Dickens' satire on grindingly slow judicial processes. In fact the £700,000 capital sum was retained, but all interest accrued during the dispute was expended. The architect really was Italian, but obscure, Chevalier Casentini of Lucca, and Englishman Philip Wilkinson executed the design. The local limestone used for the two-storey house has not proved durable.

The long 1:4:3:4:1 bay south garden front has the groups of four projecting

Brodsworth Hall, main staircase, with original carpets. RCHME

slightly and accentuated up from the parapet, but with straight cornices to the first-floor windows (the other bays having pedimented first-floor windows), and Gibbsian ground-floor windows. The east entrance front has a deeper projecting central feature, plus *porte-cochère*. Urns articulate the balustraded parapet. The terraced and statued gardens are in character.

The interior is remarkable on a number of counts. It was designed to display a large statuary collection, included an unusually large amount of circulation space, and is complete with original furniture, fittings, gadgets and decorations. In the centre of the house are a succession of display areas: entrance hall, staircase hall, marble corridor and pillared garden hall, their walls painted to imitate marbles, the floors set with Minton tiles. Surviving carpets were specially woven, in two different qualities, to match these tiles, and to fit in one piece the monumental staircase. The main ground-floor rooms, with original painted ceilings, wall damasks and furniture are considered to be the most intact surviving rooms of the period in the country.

Plate 1   *Whitby Abbey. Watercolour by John Hutchinson.*

Plate 2 *Maiden Castle from the air*. ROBERT WHITE/YORKSHIRE DALES NATIONAL PARK

Plate 3 *York Minster from the city walls.* JB

Plate 4 *Fountains Abbey, the undercroft of the lay brothers' range.* JB

Plate 5 *Easby Abbey, domestic ranges from the south. Watercolour by John Hutchinson.*

Plate 6 *Rievaulx Abbey, the church from the liturgical south-west. Watercolour by John Hutchinson.*

Plate 7 *Conisbrough Castle keep.* JB

Plate 8 *Scarborough Castle, the east face of the keep.* EH

Plate 9 *(Left) Duncombe, Park, the Old Father Time sundial on the terrace.* JB

Plate 10 *(Right) Sledmere Hall, the staircase.* JB

Plate 11 (Above) *Castle Howard, the Mausoleum from the west.* JB

Plate 12 (Below) *Temple Newsam, Chinese wallpaper.* TEMPLE NEWSAM

Plate 13 (Right) *Hull, Trinity House School.* JB

65

Burton Agnes Old Hall and Burton Agnes Hall, Humberside
12th and 17th century

TA 103633. Burton Agnes, on A166 Driffield–Bridlington road

[A] Old Hall EH

The Old Hall, an 1170s manor house, has within a round doorway a vaulted undercroft, thick chamfered ribs carried on water-leaf capitals on short round piers. A corner spiral staircase leads to the first-floor hall, with fragments of Norman and Gothic windows, and 15th-century roof timbers. The south and east elevations are encased in 17th-century brickwork with stone quoins and early 18th-century double-chamfered sash window surrounds, but the north and west sides reveal typical 12th-century stonework, and the corbelled hall chimney. The wheel of a donkey-engine was used to draw well water.

The new hall was built 1601–10 for Sir Henry Griffith (died 1620), member of the Council of the North from 1599. The surviving drawing of architect Robert Smythson differs little from the built plan, a square enclosing a central courtyard, in brick with stone dressings. The showy south front has a central range with gabled projecting end wings, but further subsidiary projections, of various shapes and roof-lines, give a vibrant effect.

The end wings have full-height bay windows, semicircular to front, canted to outer sides. The central range has, flanking a central gable, two strap-work-topped square tower-like projections, that to the left forming a porch, an ingenious device that keeps elevation symmetrical and entry logical. A second-floor long gallery gives this front three storeys. The two-storey north front has a central canted bay and square end bays. The roof-scape is enlivened by typically Elizabethan tall clustered chimneys.

The tower porch leads into the screens passage, with the amazing great hall leading off to the right. The wooden screen consists of two round arches between paired Ionic columns, entablature carved with the Twelve Tribes of Israel; in plaster bas-relief above three figured tiers – four Evangelists, Twelve Apostles, angels, knight and Elizabethan ladies. The equally immense alabaster chimney-piece is carved with Wise and Foolish Virgins. The front east wing drawing room has sumptuous round-arched panelling between pilasters, downward tapering on the upper tier. The chimney-piece has caryatids, and its main panel features a cavorting skeleton in the Dance of Death. Next is a small sitting room known as the Chinese Room from the lacquer wall panels. The Georgian dining room is in the north-east corner.

The memorable oak staircase has wide flights, carved strings, supported on paired newel posts connected by round arches, balusters symmetrically shaped about their central point, with same vase-like form above and below. On the first-floor landing are Ionic pilasters, and eight-panel doors with matching linings. In the upper drawing room Impressionist paintings hang on large bolection-edged panels. A dressing room with inserted painted linen-fold panelling is flanked by bedrooms with Jacobean fittings – in the King's, arcaded panelling and rib ceiling; in the Queen's, geometric panelling and frieze and ceiling over-run with foliage. The elegant long gallery is a tribute to those

Burton Agnes Old Hall, with the church of St Martin behind. EH

responsible for reconstruction in 1951–74.

Formal yews people the lawn between house and gatehouse, and the latter is a very fine period piece, with arms of James I, flanked by caryatids, over the round entrance archway, and corner turrets topped by ogee-shaped lead domes. In the parish church of St Martin are many monuments to owners of the halls.

66

Castle Howard, N Yorkshire
17th–18th century

SE 715700. 5 miles (8 km) SW of Malton, approached by either B1257 Helmsley–Malton road, or A64 York–Malton road

[A]

The northern approach via Coneysthorpe, preferably with Baroque music playing on the car cassette, gives a fairy-tale view of the north front across the lake. Whichever route is taken, the excitement builds: along lime avenues, with glimpse of pyramid here, obelisk there, mock fortifications or triumphal gateway. The house is kept mercifully clear of cars as visitors approach through John Carr's graceful 1781 stable block, now the Costume Galleries. A five-minute walk, or novelty train ride, reaches the house.

Charles Howard, 3rd Earl of Carlisle, powerful Whig courtier and First Lord of the Treasury, decided to rebuild Henderskelfe Castle, damaged by fire in 1693. After an unhappy episode with Comptroller of His Majesty's Works William Talman, Carlisle appointed a most unlikely architect, a former soldier enjoying success as a playwright. In 1699 John Vanbrugh was fifteen years off knighthood, but Carlisle knew him in that exclusive Whig nobility coterie the Kit Cat Club, and they clearly enjoyed each other's company.

Thus – after only theatrical design experience – Castle Howard amazingly became Vanbrugh's first architectural composition, with assistance in the practicalities of construction from the self-effacing Nicholas Hawksmoor. The

Castle Howard, the south front in 1925, before fire gutted the dome. CL

ambitious design, shown in *Vitruvius Britannicus*, was a two-storey nine-bay central block surmounted by a dome, flanked by single-storey wings to the south, and to the north a court formed by quadrant links and projecting wings with central lanterns. To the east and west there were to be kitchen and stable courts.

The central block with south wings, east wing and kitchen court were built and much landscaping achieved before Vanbrugh died in 1726. A west wing added by Sir Thomas Robinson, the 3rd Earl's architect son-in-law, only finished internally *c*.1800, was altered in 1870–5. In 1940, while an evacuated girls' school was occupying Castle Howard, fire destroyed the dome and gutted most of the south side of the building.

Visitors enter by the west wing basement. Near the foot of the top-lit grand 1870s staircase is the marble altar from behind which the Delphic Oracle is said to have prophesied, and below a Roman Doric frieze on the main landing are cabinets of superb china. Bedrooms precede a right-angled turn into the groin-vaulted passage housing Roman sculpture, cinerary urns and funerary inscriptions.

Vanbrugh's grand staircase is only glimpsed *en route* to his magnificent great hall, immensely theatrical and

theatrically immense, the brilliantly scaled space, with giant Corinthian order, much taller than the dimensions in plan. Wrought-iron balconies suggest high-level corridors, one of the devices creating a sense of space 'off-stage'. Scagliola was first used for the Baroque fireplace and statue niche opposite. Giovanni Antonio Pellegrini's *trompe-l'oeil* paintings miraculously survive on pendentives and walls; that on the dome is a 1962–3 restoration by Canadian Scott Medd.

Felix Kelly's panels in the south garden hall show new imaginary Vanbrughian follies, the next room to the west has exhibition panels of house and landscape, then three rooms have fine wood-carved Vanbrugh doors, fireplaces and cornices. From the museum room, with Venetian and tripartite windows, is a view down Robinson's west wing groin-vaulted long gallery. The space, with wonderful floor boards, opens out into a central octagon, with Holbein portraits of Henry VIII and Thomas Howard, 3rd Duke of Norfolk: juxtaposed at the north end are pictures of Castle Howard, and the Roman ruins which inspired it.

Double Composite columns and coffered ceiling from Charles Heathcote Tatham's dining hall of *c*.1800 survive in the Anglican chapel, converted and

redecorated in 1870–5. Pedimented windows have internal stained glass shutters designed by Burne-Jones, executed by William Morris: over similar quality dado panelling on the inner wall are paintings by Kempe pupils. A marble reredos successfully completes the near-Byzantine Italianate effect.

The ghost of Henderskelfe village street appears as the straight path leading south-west from the south terrace to the Temple of the Four Winds, Vanbrugh's last work, executed in 1724–6. The dome-surmounted central cube, with corner urns, and Ionic portico each side, sits on a rusticated podium extending out as entrance steps. Glazed doors allow glimpses of Francesco Vassalli's interior plasterwork. In the vista beyond is the superlative mausoleum (not open to the public). Daniel Garrett's serpentine bastion supports Hawksmoor's chapel, a solid drum with shallow dome, within a Tuscan colonnade so closely spaced it might take off into heavenly orbit. Begun in 1731, but completed after Lord Carlisle died in 1738, it is a noble monument also to Hawksmoor, who had died in 1736.

Between the two temples the rustic New River Bridge is actually a dam between two sections of an 18th-century group of informal ponds. The long and important history of Castle Howard's water gardens began up behind a bastion wall east of the house in Ray Wood, a star-shaped labyrinth once with cascades and statues, where a huge circular cistern, carved with water creatures and vegetation, feeds the south lake and its water jets. The great lake to the north was created in the 1790s, and modified by Nesfield in 1850. Nesfield also designed the circular pond within the south formal garden, with central Atlas fountain.

67

Cusworth Hall, S Yorkshire
18th century

SE 545038. Doncaster. 2 miles (3.2 km) NW of town, and 1 mile (1.6 km) W of A635 road from Doncaster NW to A1(M)

[A]

Rotherham architect George Platt designed the main house at Cusworth in 1740 and a few years later James Paine supervised internal decoration and added the south pavilions. A north court is formed by three-bay quadrant screen walls connecting the house to one-and-a-half-storey five-bay service wings, with central Gibbs-surround doorways and small pediments, and hipped roofs. In local magnesian limestone, the house is a pleasing 2:2:2-bay composition, the ground floor on a basement, the top one-and-a-half storeys above a band. Tuscan pilasters are rusticated to ground floor, the pedimented centre has Venetian openings.

Cusworth Hall, Joseph Rose plasterwork in the chapel sanctuary. RCHME

The similar 2:3:2-bay south garden front has a central segmental-pedimented ground-floor window with balustraded apron. Single-storey recessed bays link the main block to Paine's pavilions, pedimented and with round-arched openings, the centre a tall window, flanked by niches.

Now the Museum of South Yorkshire Life, the gracious interior has good plasterwork. The entrance hall has a Doric screen to the corridor crossing between two staircases, the main one with alternating column-on-vase turned balusters in pairs. A good cornice, pedimented and voluted overmantel, and doors with egg-and-dart carving, bolection frieze and pediment are in the central ground-floor room. The first-floor corridor has pedimented door-cases with pulvinated friezes, and Ionic pilasters.

The chapel in the west pavilion has excellent plasterwork by Joseph Rose of York. The sanctuary, in an externally canted niche, is separated by a beautiful Ionic screen. Opposite a splendid Venetian window is a fireplace, Ionic columns line the walls, and the ceiling has a painting of the Ascension by Francis Hayman. Less sumptuous is the east pavilion billiard room, once the dining room.

68

Duncombe Park and Rievaulx Terrace, N Yorkshire
18th century

Duncombe Park SE 603829. Less than 1 mile (1.6 km) SW of Helmsley, signposted from the town

[A]

Rievaulx Terrace SE 578844. 1 mile (1.6 km) W of B1257 Helmsley–Stokesley road, 2 miles (3.2 km) NW of Helmsley

[A] NT

The Visitor Centre contains a good model of the house, built for Thomas Duncombe to a design published in 1715 in the first volume of *Vitruvius Britannicus*. Gentleman architect

Rievaulx Terrace, Ionic temple. NT

William Wakefield, from Huby Hall near Easingwold, was clearly much influenced by Sir John Vanbrugh, whose Castle Howard (66, NY) was still being built. Most of the interiors, however, date from William Young's 1895 rebuilding, after a major fire in 1879.

Duncombe Park, in sombre brown stone, is joyless. The main west front consists of two-storey house on basement, quadrant-linked to single-storey flanking projections, between which span railings and cylindrical columns with ball finials. The eleven-bay house has a central pediment with attic, and corner turrets above paired Tuscan pilasters. The east garden front has a Roman Doric portico, heraldry in the tympanum above deep entablature, and rounded ground-floor windows: projecting end pavilions have pedimented ground-floor windows, eared and shouldered architraves above.

The two-storey ashlar west entrance hall has three bays of giant Corinthian three-quarter columns on each side, two fireplaces, round-arched panels capped by languid figures, and a flat ceiling painted as if domed. The saloon to the east, the length of the central range, with at each end Ionic screens, pedimented doorways flanked by shell niches, and acanthus frieze, is kept rather bare to provide a small auditorium. Wall panelling, despite gilded acanthus borders and ribboned garlands, sustains the brown theme.

Gold damask in the south withdrawing room provides welcome

relief, and this room contains a white marble fireplace, deep plaster frieze and good ceiling. The north dining room has dark red walls and carpet, pale green curtains, and Corinthian screen. The ladies' withdrawing room has acanthus frieze, coved ceiling and corner fireplace. The library, hardly light enough to read in, mainly contains estate ledgers. The stone staircase has a wrought-iron balustrade.

Near the house are Victorian gardens: the main landscape is of Charles Bridgeman's period. Father Time holding a sundial, attributed to John van Nost, draws the eye across a large croquet lawn to the gently curved terrace, and to the distant vistas down into the valley of the Rye. At each end of the terrace stands a temple, to the south a Doric drum reminiscent of Stowe's Ancient Virtue, and to the north an Ionic rotunda open to the moors beyond. Return to the house past the terrace end supported by a serpentine bastion, through a spooky yew walk: the trees of Duncombe Park are magnificent.

In 1754–8 a later Thomas Duncombe added a second terrace and temples at Rievaulx 2 miles to the north-west (as a crow flies). The concept is now subtly more romantic: the terrace edges are tree-softened, vistas down into the valley ever-changing, and Rievaulx Abbey (25, NY) is a splendid eye-catcher. The rectangular Ionic temple contains a banqueting room, surprisingly rich inside, with furniture by William Kent, and ceiling painted by Giovanni Borgnis. In case of chilly weather, there is a white marble fireplace with caryatids and an overmantel with scrolled pediment. At the other end is the Doric rotunda, with shallow dome, internally coffered and painted.

69
East Riddlesden Hall, W Yorkshire
17th century

SE 079421. East Riddlesden. S of A650 Keighley–Bingley road, 1 mile (1.6 km) E of Keighley

[A] NT

An Edwardian photograph of East Riddlesden Hall. The now-ruined range is shown on the right, still complete. BRADFORD LIBRARIES

A West Riding yeoman house of the 1640s, built for wealthy Halifax clothier James Murgatroyd, was added to in 1692 by his grandson Edmund Starkie. The plan of East Riddlesden Hall is not immediately apparent from the north approach. To the right lie the ruins of Starkie's range, a mere elevation with low ground-floor windows, tall first-floor cross windows with pediments, and three gables with oculi and ball finials above. In the centre a low and rather plain range called the Banqueting Hall is really the great hall, with cross-passage to left. To the left again is Murgatroyd's everyday living quarters, a double-bay range with kitchen and individual rooms.

At each end of the cross-passage is a castellated tower porch, with wheel window above round-arched doorway flanked by fluted acanthus columns, and a seated vestibule. The domestic rooms have very large mullioned-and-transomed windows, with king mullions every three lights. Inside, the much-restored banqueting hall has an original fireplace with entablature. Across the passage is the kitchen. To its east the

oak-panelled dining room has a pomegranate plaster frieze and rib ceiling. The south-facing drawing room, also panelled, has heraldic devices in the panels of its rib ceiling, and a fireplace with inlaid overmantel, also the date *1648* and an enigmatic inscription. First-floor rooms also have good contemporary fittings.

A garden wall to the south contains bee-boles. Obscuring part of the north facade is a castellated service range with elaborately shaped door-heads, one dated *1642* with Murgatroyd initials, and the inscription *Vive le Roy*, which history would shortly prove ironic. A farm building, now a comfort station, also has ornate doorways, slit vent windows, and more bee-boles.

Of the two large barns beside the drive, the Airedale Barn has recessed wain entry and round-arched vents. The internal timber structure of the Great Barn is aisled, the posts set on stone bases. The light slits are arched, with trefoil effect, and inside are piscina-like lantern niches. There are two pairs of entrances, with round-arched recessed porches.

70

Ebberston Hall, N Yorkshire
18th century

SE 892833. Ebberston. 5 miles
(8 km) E of Pickering on N side of
A170 Pickering–Scarborough road,
just W of village

[A]

No less an architect than Colen
Campbell designed this miniature
stately home, built in 1718 for William
Thompson, Member of Parliament for
Scarborough, and Ebberston is
illustrated in the third volume of
Vitruvius Britannicus. Originally with
central cupola and pavilions with
quadrant links, the main block now
forms a tiny three-bay villa, apparently
of one storey, with on the south front an
imposing flight of stone steps, leading to
a terrace, its vermiculated front with
shell niches, concealing a large
basement, where much of the
accommodation is situated.

Built of ashlar sandstone which has
weathered badly, the *piano nobile* has
vermiculated rustication. The central
doorway has round-arched head with
radial fanlight between attached Tuscan
columns, smooth but for projecting
bands of frosted rustication, carrying a
pediment with bust in the tympanum.
The sash windows have flat arches. All
three openings have exaggerated
voussoirs and dropped keystones carved
with a human head, that of the door also
having William Thompson's ligatured
initials, those to the windows a lion's
mask at embarrassingly close distance.
The balustraded parapet has corner
urns. The five-bay north elevation is of
two storeys, with a first-floor central
three-bay Tuscan loggia, originally
open.

Inside the stone-floored entrance hall
the front door-case is a segmental
pediment on Doric entablature into
which the fanlight encroaches. A similar
doorway, but with complete entablature,
forms the entrance to the former loggia,
now the dining room, with Ionic
pilasters and a rich frieze.

The rooms, though small, are
carefully proportioned. The doors are
tall and narrow, the surrounds with
acanthus carving. Some woodwork is of
high quality, probably by William
Thornton. Left of the entrance the
drawing room has bolection panelling,
fireplace framed by Corinthian pilasters

and flanked by cupboards, rich frieze
decorated with dragons, coved cornice.
The tiny room behind has a fleur-de-lis
frieze. To the right are two bedrooms,
one with bolection-moulded fireplace,
and cornice with egg-and-dart motif and
paired modillions with acanthus in-
between.

The open loggia was intended to
provide a view of the formally-classical
water garden, one of the first Italianate
gardens created in England. Behind the
house are the remains of three pools
separated by cascades: running further
up the wooded valley was a long canal.

71

Hackfall, N Yorkshire
18th century

SE 235772. Grewelthorpe, 6 miles
(9.6 km) NW of Ripon and 4 miles
(6.4 km) W of North Stainley (via
A6108 Ripon–West Tanfield road).
From Grewelthorpe, ¼ mile
(0.4 km) along footpath leading NE

[D] LT and The Woodland Trust

William Aislabie, who completed his
father's more formal landscape a few
miles away at Studley Royal (78, NY),
created Hackfall's highly dramatic
landscape from 1748. Much celebrated
in its day, it is particularly important on
two counts: it utilised, and hardly
altered, the outstanding natural beauty
of the site; and it was not attached to a
country house, a contributory factor to
its subsequent neglect.

The name Hackfall refers to a
tributary waterfall, tumbling in a craggy
wooded gorge, to meet the River Ure in a
secluded and idyllically rocky spot.
Hanging woods in the valley were subtly
thinned and planted, to reveal, then
obscure, views of both streams, and
occasional scars of rock.

Strategically placed follies included a
half-octagonal rustic temple of massive
stones, and Fisher Hall, an octagonal
pavilion with Gothick opening in each
side, revealing splendid views, named
after Studley's long-serving gardener
William Fisher. Aislabie added
Fountains Abbey (18, NY) to Studley and

Ebberston Hall. CL

Hackfall, Mowbray Castle. LT

named two follies at Hackfall after Roger de Mowbray, patron of Fountains: Mowbray Castle – an ovoid sham fortification with Gothick openings and crenellations, and internal Egyptian pillars, built on the edge of Hackfall

Woods – and Mowbray Point.

Mowbray Point, Hackfall's most significant building, combined the roles of eye-catcher and banqueting house, and was therefore placed in the most accessible part of the landscape. Approached across a flat field it appears to be a small Palladian villa with central pediment, except that some windows have Gothick heads; inside are ogee niches. Visible above the banqueting house roof, and meant to be seen to more dramatic effect from the other side, through the woods hanging below it, are elevated vaults suggestive of the ruins of Roman *thermae*.

Hackfall has for many years been perceived merely as a wood from which occasionally to harvest a cash crop of timber. Now the Woodland Trust is recreating the walks from which this sublimely picturesque landscape can be enjoyed, and the Landmark Trust is restoring Mowbray Point.

72
Harewood House, W Yorkshire
18th century

SE 311446. Harewood. Entrance from village, opposite junction of A61 Leeds–Harrogate road and A659 Wetherby road, 7 miles (11.2 km) N of Leeds

[A]

In 1759 Edwin Lascelles, Whig Member of Parliament, used West Indian sugar money to begin his new palace, built in the estate's beautiful honey-coloured sandstone to plans by John Carr of York. In 1765 Robert Adam was brought in to do the interiors, for which the best craftsmen and materials were used. The rusticated basement of the Palladian design shows only on the south garden

Harewood House, south front. CL

front, made more Italianate by Sir Charles Barry in 1843.

The north front's main two-storey nine-bay block has giant order Corinthian attached columns carrying a five-bay pediment with coat of arms, windows to the *piano nobile* with alternate triangular and segmental pediments, smaller square windows above, and balustraded parapet with urns. Single-storey three-bay ranges link to end pavilions, each with Venetian window.

In the north entrance hall, with dark red marble free Doric half-columns, deliberately punning Adam's name, stands Jacob Epstein's 1939 statue of the first man. To the left the Corinthian-pilastered old library has a coved ceiling by Joseph Rose, the second of two ante-rooms a dome with coats of arms, blue frieze and apsed fireplace with blue shafts to Ionic columns.

On the east side Edwin Lascelles' bedroom has an Adam ceiling, on the south front one sitting room contains a blue fireplace; another, hung with green silk, has a bed-alcove with Ionic columns; the drawing room has a fine Adam ceiling. From the central saloon, later the library, apsed towards the entrance hall, its two white marble fireplaces with columned and pedimented overmantels, there is an enfilade of doors along the south front. Another drawing-room ceiling has Victorian colouring; the former south dining room has a Victorian ceiling with *trompe-l'oeil* centre-piece.

The gallery along the west side, altered by Barry, was restored in 1989–90 to Adam's design, reinstating the white marble Nollekens fireplace, with draped posing caryatids. There is specially made flock wallpaper, and over the end and central Venetian windows, with dark green Ionic columns, are panels carved by Chippendale and painted as *trompe-l'oeil* drapes. Large pier mirrors between the windows make the space even lighter.

Turning into the north side, one enters the dining room with its Barry monogrammed coved ceiling, the large white marble fireplace he put in the gallery, and fine mahogany doors. The original Adam music-room carpet

mirrors the ceiling, with roundels painted by Angelica Kauffman: large classical scenes by Antonio Zucchi adorn the walls, with decorative plaster panels.

Edwin Lascelles commissioned 'Capability' Brown to landscape the park, costing £6,000 over eight years from 1772; to the south a lake, carefully placed clumps and belts of trees, another vista to natural Almscliff Crag, 4 miles (6.4 km) to the north-west beyond Harewood Bank. There is the ruined Harewood Castle, crenellated in 1367 by William Lord Aldburgh. His daughters Elizabeth and Sibilla married into the Redman and Ryther families, who held Harewood until the late 16th century. Gawthorp, seat of the Gascoignes, was also in the parish.

A new village, designed by John Carr in 1760, was built on the turnpike road: sole survivor of the old is the Church of All Saints of c.1410, which is vested in the Redundant Churches Fund. Its six extremely fine Derbyshire alabaster tombs, still with traces of brightly coloured paint, illustrate late 15th and early 16th-century fashion changes in male armour and female dress and accessories: they are here described in anti-clockwise order, beginning in the south aisle.

Sir William Gascoigne (died 1487) wears a short-sleeved tabard over his armour; his wife Margaret, daughter of Henry Percy, 3rd Earl of Northumberland, wears a widow's veil; the chest has weepers in nodding ogee arches. The knight's helmet of Sir William Gascoigne (died c.1465) has a pike's head, the Gascoigne crest; his wife, Margaret Clarell of Aldwark, also has widow's veil; their chest smaller ogee niches for fifteen weepers. The oldest tomb is Sir William Gascoigne (died 1419), Lord Chief Justice, in judicial robes and coif, lying beside his first wife, Elizabeth Mowbray of Kirklington, their chest with angels carrying shields.

In an arch between chancel and Gascoigne south chapel are Sir William Ryther (died 1425) and wife Sybilla Aldburgh; her sister Elizabeth lies in the equivalent north arch, with Sir Richard Redman of Levens (died 1426). Both

sisters have elaborate head-dresses, both husbands similar plate armour and large gauntlets. In the north chapel long-haired Sir Edward Redman (died 1510), in plainer armour, has a small bedesman by his foot; his wife Elizabeth Huddlestone (died 1529), wears a draped wimple and full-sleeved dress; in crocketed ogee niches below are their children, shown as weepers, and saints identified by their appropriate symbols.

73

Kiplin Hall, N Yorkshire
17th century

SE 274975. Kiplin, S of B6271 Richmond–Northallerton road, 2½ miles (4 km) SE of Scorton

[A]

Sir George Calvert (c.1578–1632), Secretary of State to James I in 1619–25, was in 1625 created 1st Lord Baltimore in the Irish Peerage, and in 1632 was granted land by Charles I to found a colony in America. Maryland, named in honour of the Queen, Henrietta Maria, was a free state, with greater religious toleration than most, particularly for Roman Catholics.

About 1620 Calvert had built Kiplin Hall, a three-storey house in brick with diaper decoration, the plan severely symmetrical. Turrets, topped by ogee domes, project from the centre of each side of an almost-square rectangle. The flanking walls are gabled, there are string courses, and the windows have cross mullions and transoms.

One turret is a tower porch, and two

Kiplin Hall from the west. JH

turrets originally contained staircases. Inside the main house, the longer axis is bisected by a spine wall, housing flues, pierced on the top floor across the shorter axis by a long gallery extending into the turret rooms. The interior was remodelled in the second quarter of the 18th century by Christopher Crowe, who inserted a grander staircase. In 1820 Peter Frederick Robinson added to the south side a Gothick drawing room, remodelled later as an Elizabethan library by William Eden Nesfield, who also landscaped the grounds.

74

Newby Hall, N Yorkshire
17th–18th century

SE 347674. Off B6265 Ripon–Boroughbridge road 3 miles (4.8 km) SE of Ripon, 1 mile (1.6 km) SW of small village of Skelton-on-Ure

[A]

This house was built in the 1690s by Sir Edward Blackett, Member of Parliament for Ripon, then sold in 1748 to Richard Weddell, whose son William went on a Grand Tour in 1765–6, and returned with a collection of Roman sculpture, and a set of Gobelins tapestries on order. To display these he altered the three-storey 3:3:3-bay house, and added to its east front two-storey wings designed by John Carr. Robert Adam decorated the interiors. William Weddell's cousin, the 3rd Lord Grantham, added a regency dining room, above which a billiard room was put by Robert Vyner, son of his younger daughter Mary, whose other son Frederick was murdered by Greek brigands.

The 1690s block is in small orange-red brick with stone dressings. The sides are of 2:1:2 bays, the west garden front 2:2:1:2:2 bays: each elevation with a quietly emphasised central feature. The tall sash windows, with crown glass, are some of the earliest known. The east entrance hall stone floor reflects the Adam ceiling above, and is by the younger Joseph Rose, as are the plaster wall panels depicting military trophies. Fluted-panel mahogany doors are

Newby Hall, Gobelins tapestry. RCHME

arranged symmetrically in the corners.

The drawing room to the north was originally the library. The regency dining room has segmental-arched alcoves, their soffits with plaster rosettes in recessed panels, and frieze with urns and lions' masks. A Victorian staircase leads to a number of pretty bedrooms, including a circular one with painted panels and ceiling copied from Herculaneum in Chinese style.

On the main staircase, of wood with delicate cast-iron balustrades, hangs Pompeo Batoni's portrait of William Weddell. The staircase ground-floor ante-room has magnificent Ionic columns of blue Cipollino marble. Adam excelled himself in the tapestry room: the doors have guilloche motif panels, the friezes of their cases Ionic flutes, each with acanthus bud; the Adam ceiling has roundels painted by Antonio Zucchi. The splendid dining room which Adam designed for William Weddell,

with Corinthian screens to the end carving apses, is now a library; there is a very large fireplace, and delightful plasterwork by Joseph Rose.

Carr's south wing is the sculpture gallery, divided into three rooms, the central one Pantheon-based: some Roman statues have added fig-leaves, and a huge marble sarcophagus at the far end is misnamed a Roman bath. The large and much cherished gardens are embarrassingly immaculate. York architect William Bellwood designed the ashlar sandstone stable block, and good entrance lodges in Skelton village.

Here is the Church of Christ the Consoler, built using the ransom raised for the release of Frederick Grantham Vyner, who was shot in 1870 at the age of twenty-three, by his party's Greek brigand captors, when they saw Greek troops bringing the money to them. Externally the church, with chancel, aisled nave and tall spire, is similar to that of St Mary, Studley Royal (39, NY), also designed by William Burges for the same family, though here the architect has created a much more sorrowful atmosphere – even the churchyard trees are weeping varieties.

75

Nostell Priory, W Yorkshire
18th century

SE 404175. Wragby, N of A638 Wakefield–Doncaster road, 5 miles (8 km) SE of Wakefield

[A] NT

The house was built for the Winn family on a medieval priory site in honey-hued ashlar sandstone from 1735, and Colonel James Moyser's Palladian design was implemented from 1736 by the young James Paine, who thus settled locally. His interiors have sumptuous rococo plasterwork, probably by Thomas Perritt and the elder Joseph Rose. Another phase, with the younger Rose's plasterwork and Thomas Chippendale's furniture – still in the house – was begun c.1765 by Robert Adam, who also

added a north-east family wing, stables and other ancillary buildings.

The east front's main 5:5:5 bay block should have had four quadrant wings, but only one, for kitchens, was built. Paine's giant-order attached Ionic columns carry a pediment with Winn arms in tympanum; the *piano nobile* windows have alternating triangular and segmental pediments. To the right Adam's exquisite 1:3:1-bay wing, with Ionic portico and tactfully recessed link, is unmatched to the left, so the composition is asymmetrical, but the rusticated basement unifies.

A small door in the external perron below Paine's portico goes into the ashlar low basement hall, with Holbein picture of Sir Thomas More's family and Georgian doll's house amazingly similar to the house. Of the two fine cantilevered stone staircases with wrought-iron balustrades, that of 1747 to the south is seen first, top-lit by lantern on coffered cornice, the plasterwork richer nearer the light, flowing rococo shields in oddly-shaped panels.

The lofty top hall, once entered from the portico, rolls the decorative clock

forward twenty-seven years: Adam's superb Roman-inspired plasterwork includes lunette panels above openings, and hemisphere at inner side. Round lobbies on the west side of the top hall connect it to the saloon and both staircases. The north staircase plasterwork is yet more splendid, military with eagles and spears. Paine's Venetian window was reset when Adam extended the billiard room. His first room here (1766–7) was the ornate library, with its Ionic pilastered and pedimented bookshelves and paintings by Antonio Zucchi. Chippendale's massive table was made specially for the library, and is older-fashioned than Harewood's (72, WY) which is now at Temple Newsam (79, WY).

Next, the tapestry room has a fine Adam chimney-piece, Zucchi panels over-door and in the ceiling, otherwise repainted by Thomas Ward c.1822, when mid-18th-century Flemish tapestries were put in. To be seen in Adam's 1768 saloon are more Rose plasterwork and Zucchi paintings; Corinthian pilasters framing the top-hall niche; a deeply coved ceiling and twin marble chimney-pieces.

In rococo contrast is Paine's dining room, three-dimensional ceiling decoration with food and drink theme, (plump putti the result); caryatids flank cornucopiae on the chimney-piece, its overmantel with Baroque aedicule; door-cases have bolection friezes, and over-door panels have bow-shaped tops. End wall portraits – Palladian block builder fourth baronet Sir Rowland Winn, and his brother – have acanthus fronds wrapping around the frames.

Paine's music room – instruments on the coved ceiling include a violin projecting daringly – became the state bedchamber, with Chinese wallpaper and Thomas Chippendale green and gold lacquered chinoiserie furniture. Paine's adjacent principal bedchamber became Adam's state dressing room, its bed alcove altered with Ionic columns, and more Chinese wallpaper and chinoiserie furniture. Two rooms badly damaged by a tragic fire in 1980 have been superbly restored, with new painted fabric bed-hangings. Two bathrooms miraculously retain more Chinese wallpaper.

Nostell Priory, saloon ceiling. RCHME

76

Ormesby Hall, Cleveland
18th century

NZ 539167. Middlesbrough. 3 miles (4.8 km) SE of centre, off B1380 Eston road

[A] NT

Built *c*.1740 during the ownership of Sir James Pennyman, who died in 1743, the credit for building Ormesby is due to his wife Dorothy. She was the daughter of William Wake, an Archbishop of Canterbury renowned for building activities, who died in 1737 leaving her a substantial inheritance. The house was unoccupied from Lady Dorothy's death in 1754 until the sixth baronet, known as 'Wicked Sir James' because of extravagance, took up residence in 1770, adding to and partly redecorating the house to his rather more grandiose taste.

Rather ponderous in darkish ashlar sandstone, the two-and-a-half-storey 1:3:1-bay squarish block has a central pediment containing the family arms, and the roof, hipped because of the square plan, has somewhat random chimneys. The sash windows, graded in size from bottom to top, are plain except for keystones, and a hint of central emphasis. The more interesting interior is a mix of 1740s and 1770s work. The north-front entrance hall, of the 1740s, has at each end a screen of fluted Ionic columns, pleasing chimney-piece and decorative ceiling. Symmetrically placed mahogany doors, of six fluted panels, have door-cases with fluted cornices.

In the north-west corner is the library, also 1740s, its plaster chimney-piece with scrolled open pediment. The drawing room, in the rest of the west side, originally the dining room, with Corinthian screen to serving recess, was redone in the 1770s, and has an Adam-style ceiling and elegant chimney-piece. At the south end of the hall the original drawing room, extended by a bay window to make a dining room capable of seating a large Victorian dinner party, also has gracious decoration of the 1770s.

The stairs hall, its doorways with

Ormesby Hall, south front. NT

pulvinated friezes, is placed in the centre east side, because the elegant staircase, with three slender turned balusters to each tread, leads to a first-floor corridor on the longer axis of the house. This forms a gracious gallery, the house's most remarkable feature, with lateral screen of four columns – their capitals with palmette leaves, plasterwork wall panels and ornate cornice. The flanking rooms are entered by symmetrically placed sumptuous door-cases, all pedimented but in varying designs – broken on brackets, segmental on Corinthian pilasters, broken on Ionic pilasters. Guest rooms to the north are well fitted, with fine pedimented chimney-pieces, and a closet has a corner fireplace.

In the kitchen court a 17th-century building has a Jacobean round-arched door-case flanked by columns, with coat of arms above, re-used from the earlier house on the site. The fine stable block, a 1770s addition, probably the work of John Carr of York, is now the home of Cleveland Constabulary's horses. Of 3:3:3 bays, with round-arched ground-floor openings and small first-floor windows, the central pedimented feature has a cupola above a clock. Entrance lodges are of the same period.

77

Sledmere House, Humberside
18th and 20th century

SE 931647. Sledmere, 8 miles (12.8 km) NW of Great Driffield on B1252. S of B1252 road

[A]

This rather severe two-storey seven-bay pedimented classical house, which was rebuilt in 1751 by Richard Sykes, was inherited in 1776 by his energetic agricultural reformer nephew Sir Christopher Sykes, who had 'Capability' Brown landscape the park, and rebuilt the village. To his own design in the 1780s he gave the house an H-plan by adding large wings, and plasterer Joseph Rose transformed it inside into an elegant Georgian country seat. This survived until gutted by fire in 1911, and was then restored by Walter Brierley as a convincingly Georgian mansion, which is Edwardian in scale and grandeur.

It is built of ashlar sandstone so smooth it almost looks rendered. The entrance front, returned by Brierley to the east side, is fairly plain. Sir Christopher's south entrance front has widely spaced arched recesses containing tripartite windows, taller to first floor where the tympana have sculptured panels, divided by columns, Tuscan on the ground floor, Ionic above. The west side, rebuilt to an unexecuted design of Sir Christopher's, has giant Ionic pilasters carrying a pediment with heraldry in the tympanum.

Inside, the Edwardian plasterwork is extremely rich, some of it from re-used Georgian moulds, some rather more vibrant in character. The hall, on the east–west axis, has a Tuscan entablature, alternating metopes of elephants' heads and Tritons – from family crests – resting on columns painted like marble. The principal rooms are arranged symmetrically to north and south.

To the north, the Music Room has anthemion on pilaster panels and winged horses and lyres to frieze. Behind, a room with Ionic corner pilasters is full of horse portraits. The south drawing room has typically Rose decoration, its ceiling depicting Greek religious rites, frieze of paired mermaids holding urns, and mirrored wall panels. Behind is the red-damask-hung boudoir with chinoiserie overmantel mirror. The large west dining room ceiling, in the

manner of William Kent, survives from the 1751 house, the carving alcove with rather garish blue palmette columns matching the Chinese porcelain displayed there.

The grand imperial staircase is also on an east–west axis: the copy of the naked Apollo Belvedere in the landing alcove requires female visitors to gaze carefully at the stairs. Wrought-iron panels matching the balustrades guard doorways opening out from upper corridors: an elliptical lantern on paired Ionic columns hangs in space. A self-portrait of Joseph Rose has due prominence on the library landing, semicircular in plan and with yellow Ionic columns. The monumental library gallery occupies the whole south wing first floor, its delicately decorated ceiling reminiscent of the Roman Baths of Diocletian, with three groin-vaults separated by short tunnel-vaults; the book-cases have Ionic pilaster divisions, the floor is of beautiful marquetry.

Descent back to the ground floor takes in the wonderful Turkish room, a copy of the Sultan's room in Istanbul's Valideh Mosque, with Damascus-made brilliant blue tiles of various patterns,

and a small table and two chairs inlaid with mother-of-pearl.

The quadrangular stable block, externally in railway station yellow brick, internally red brick, has a five-bay front elevation of round arches and paired Doric columns carrying a pediment with tympanum clock, and a cupola of similar columns behind. Temple Moore's Decorated-style Church of St Mary of 1897 in the house grounds replaced one by Richard Sykes.

Outside the house entrance is the Eleanor Cross, also by Temple Moore and of 1895, but with added First World War memorial brasses. Another war memorial is to Sir Mark Sykes' Company of Waggoners, a short drum carved with war scenes in relief, and four almost-attached decorated columns. The village is consistently interesting, pleasing and charming but never twee.

Just over 2 miles (3.2 km) down the road the Sir Tatton Sykes Memorial Tower, dated 1865, built in beige stone with dark red bands, is Gothicish, with sculptured panels in niches, ligatures of the *TS* initials, and the north, south, east and west directions named. It is set within a railed enclosure surrounded by a ha-ha, and is guarded across the road by a little Gothic cottage, in similar brick colours.

78
Studley Royal, N Yorkshire
18th century

SE 2870. Studley Royal. 2 miles (3.2 km) SW of Ripon, S of B6265 Ripon–Pateley Bridge road

[A] NT

John Aislabie, Member of Parliament for Ripon, began landscaping the run-down Studley estate inherited in 1699 from his mother's family shortly before becoming Chancellor of the Exchequer in 1718. His political career was, however, short-lived, for as a leading light in the South Sea Company which collapsed spectacularly in 1720, he was dismissed from Parliament in 1721. Retiring in disgrace to his new (now-demolished) house at Studley, Aislabie devoted

Sledmere House. JB

himself to creating a fine garden until his death in 1742.

Based on French formal gardens, early 18th-century landscapes created vistas along man-made axes, harmoniously blending greenery and water, both in contrasting forms: greenery in horizontal smooth lawns and linear clipped hedges, and vertical trees in three-dimensional shapes; water in still, flat sheets, to reflect the planting and any suitably-placed eye-catching buildings or statues, and upright cascades of moving water.

Aislabie was innovative. Studley's main axis is not artificial, but the River Skell. This he canalised, but it had nevertheless to follow the meandering line of its valley which, although running generally west–east, in the Studley estate turns through two right angles to go due north before going east again. He made extensive use of evergreen trees in the planting pattern, to keep the landscape green during the winter, and he created vistas to two important medieval buildings, Ripon Cathedral (33, NY) and Fountains Abbey (18, NY), both outside the boundaries of the land he owned.

John tried and failed to purchase Fountains Abbey, but used the ruins as a Gothic eye-catcher nevertheless: it was eventually purchased by his son William, who continued landscaping from 1742 until his death in 1781. He landscaped areas both upstream and downstream of his father's garden in the softer, more romantic character fashionable by the second half of the 18th century. At the top of the long avenue giving the vista to Ripon Cathedral, William Aislabie put a pyramid monument to his father, replaced in 1805 by an obelisk, next to which was later built the Church of St Mary (39, NY).

East of the estate is a steep-sided valley, wooded by William Aislabie, who made carriage drives of fords criss-crossing the river, pedestrian bridges alongside, a route now called the Valley of the Seven Bridges. Above the great lake at its head the Skell is held by a cascade flanked by rusticated columns and fishing pavilions: to its west the Canal Gate to John Aislabie's garden.

West of the canalised Skell is a small half-moon-shaped pond and Banqueting House, probably by Colen Campbell, with richly decorated interior. High on the east side is the Gothic Temple. Below, flanked by crescent ponds, the circular moon pond: reflected in it is the Temple of Piety, originally of Hercules, renamed by William as a filial gesture soon after his father's death, its interior with plaster decoration based on Roman Doric designs.

Sound names the Drum Fall, with its changing angle and levels of canals: up in woods to the east the Doric rotunda Temple of Fame was moved here by William in 1781. A rustic bridge cascades a second canal. To its south a large half-moon pond 'bites' the artificial Tent Hill visually separating water garden and abbey ruins. John Aislabie's 'surprise view', high up in the woods to the east, glimpsed the ruins long before his son William could take his lawn right up to them.

Studley Royal, the moon pond and Temple of Piety. DARLINGTON AND STOCKTON TIMES

79

Temple Newsam, W Yorkshire
17th century

SE 356321. Leeds. 4 miles (6.4 km)
E of city centre, S of A63 Selby road
and 1 mile (1.6 km) S of Whitkirk
[A]

The site once belonged to the Knights
Templar, hence the name. In the
courtyard-plan house built *c*.1500–20,
Henry Lord Darnley, second husband of
Mary, Queen of Scots was born in 1545.
In 1622 it was sold to wealthy courtier
Sir Arthur Ingram, who demolished all
except one range, and added to it the
north and south wings extending east.
The three-storey U-plan house so
created is now a Leeds City Museum and
Art Gallery with a magnificent
collection.

In brown brick with stone dressings,
the ranges are only one room deep, but
long, giving a large amount of external
wall, and also of parapets, used for a
wordy pious and loyal inscription. The
mullioned and transomed windows form
projecting bays, and the older brickwork
of the central range incorporates a
diaper pattern. The central cupola was
added in 1788.

Entry from the court is by a tower
porch in the centre of the south wing,
into what was a screens passage, at one
end of the great hall, architecturally a
mix of many periods, but containing in
the large bay window heraldic glass,
describing early owners and painted by
Baernard Dinninckhoff. A hatchment-
hung passage leads to the Edwardian
library, housing Thomas Chippendale's
majestic library writing table made
c.1770 for Harewood House (72, WY).
The lobby and Chinese Drawing Room
have hand-painted Chinese wallpaper.

C E Kempe's 1894–7 oak staircase
leads by family apartments to the north-
wing picture gallery, converted from a
Jacobean predecessor by the 7th
Viscount Irwin in 1738–45. The
architect was Daniel Garrett, the fine

Temple Newsam House from the west. WEST PARK STUDIOS

early Georgian plasterwork by Thomas
Perritt and Joseph Rose senior, of York.
The ceiling contains royal family
portrait reliefs; two chimney-pieces,
with caryatid busts set at angles,
overmantel pictures and scrolled broken
pediments on Ionic columns, based on
designs by William Kent; at each end are
pedimented door-cases; the window
shutters are beautifully carved. Almost
all James Pascall's original furniture
survives here. The contemporary library
has Corinthian columns and a more
three-dimensional floriate ceiling.

On the second floor, a south-wing
corridor houses a collection of historic
wallpaper and hangings; and the west-
range Tudor Room has linen-fold
panelling and built-in furniture of
c.1530, contemporary with the building,
and also a deep plaster frieze of strapwork and naturalistic forms. The north-
west corner 1790s stone staircase has a
delicate wrought-iron balustrade.

Displays in the outbuildings include a
section on the garden history of Temple
Newsam, the park having been
landscaped by 'Capability' Brown.

The Church of St Mary, Whitkirk has
many fine monuments. At the south
aisle west end that to Charles Viscount
Irwin (died 1778) and wife Frances (died
1807) has a sorrowing female figure with
urn. A large wall monument in the 1448
south chantry chapel to Edward Lord
Viscount Ingram in the Kingdom of
Scotland (died 1688) shows him looking
away from his wife Elizabeth's weeping
figure towards that of his daughter, with
skull in hand, who died aged two. In a
Tudor arch recline elegantly clad
alabaster figures of Sir Robert Scargill
(died 1532) and his wife, the weepers
between classical columns. North
chancel wall monuments include that to
engineer John Smeaton FRS (died
1792), with a sculpture of his famous
'Edystone [*sic*]' lighthouse.

7

Villages, Towns and Cities

The settlements in this chapter have been chosen to represent the variety in the region, and the coverage is by no means exhaustive. Among the cities **York** (95, NY) has the longest history, and was the 'Capital of the North'. It will probably also achieve a place in modern history for its phenomenal growth as a tourist attraction in the last quarter of the 20th century. The continuing history of **Hull** (87, H) as a seaport goes back to medieval times. The fine market place of the small city of Ripon is mentioned in chapter 3 under Ripon Cathedral (33, NY).

Northern England is to many people synonymous with industry, and three industrial towns have been chosen, both for their fine buildings and the historical development they represent. **Halifax** (84, WY) was very important in the hand-powered and early water-powered eras of cloth production, and also has two important model villages of industrial housing. **Bradford** (81, WY) demonstrates the grandeur of the steam-powered era, and represents the British zenith of international trade. **Leeds** (88, WY) is very much the provincial commercial capital of the region.

Heptonstall (30, WY), an early textile community which developed organically in a difficult location, is mentioned briefly in chapter 3. Included in chapter 8 is Saltaire (106, WY), another model settlement. It is somewhere between village and town in size and the facilities it offers, and has everything but a parish church – although the large Congregational Church fills that role visually – and the huge textile mill is almost like a vast feudal mansion.

The coast features directly or indirectly in several of the settlements selected. **Scarborough** (93, NY) has a long history as a coastal defence and a port, and then became first a spa and later a seaside resort. **Goole** (83, H) lies inland but because of its good links to the sea, and thence the London markets, was purpose-built as a coal port. **Saltburn** (92, C) was also deliberately developed, but for different reasons – as a new seaside town. **Whitby** (94, NY) is a seaside settlement of great charm, as are Staithes, Robin Hood's Bay and Runswick Bay. **Harrogate** (85, NY), although inland, is another leisure resort, and was also consciously developed, as a major spa.

(*Left*) York, city walls and Minster. EH

(*Right*) Manningham Mills, Bradford. RCHME

Among small towns **Richmond** (90, NY) is very special, having extensive history, and a wide variety of interesting buildings for its size, but above all having in full measure that quality of the picturesque which the early Gothick Revivalists so cherished. **Beverley** (80, H) has attractive Georgian streets and magnificent churches. Stokesley, which is also very attractive, and Yarm, important for its history as an early port, are also rewarding to visit.

The two old villages selected, **Coxwold** (82, NY) and **Heath** (86, WY), though both organic in development pattern, are of contrasting forms, Coxwold linear, Heath peripheral to a surprisingly large open space. The planned villages of **Ripley** (91, NY) and **New Earswick** (89, NY) are also very different in character, Ripley being an existing village redesigned in a romantic French-inspired style, and New Earswick an early example of a completely new 'garden' settlement inspired by strong political ideals. Baldersby St James – of the 1850s, falling between the two in date – is not included but provides an interesting comparison, as it represents a different political ideal: the Victorian image of a medieval village as perceived by the Oxford Movement. Two more interesting estate villages mentioned in chapter 6 are Harewood (72, WY) and Sledmere (77, H). The remarkable deserted village of Wharram Percy (11, NY) is not considered a living settlement and so is included in chapter 1.

80

Beverley, Humberside

7 miles (11.2 km) NW of Kingston upon Hull and 8½ miles (13.6 km) N of Humber estuary, via major roads

One of England's most prosperous medieval towns, Beverley had by the 13th century a defensive ditch with four gates or bars. The ditch was never replaced by a wall, but the North Bar was rebuilt in 1409 in hand-made bricks (small and irregular in size, dark brown in colour), the Humberside area being among the first in the country thus to

Beverley, North Bar Without. HMK

utilise local clays. Both faces of the North Bar have small windows, statue niches, shields, and courses of decorative brickwork carry the elaborately crenellated parapet. The gates remain inside the outer arch, there is a portcullis slot within the inner arch, and between are two bays of rib vaulting.

In a nearby street called North Bar Within is the beautiful guild Church of St Mary, large, Perpendicular, of cruciform plan with generous transepts, crossing tower and clerestories. The fine west front with projecting turrets pierced at the top (reminiscent of King's College Chapel, Cambridge but a century older), is set off by splendid 18th-century wrought-iron gates.

The nave, narrow like its aisleless 12th-century predecessor, is mostly late work of 1524, for major reconstruction followed the 1520 central tower collapse. Local residents who contributed to repairs are commemorated in portrait head label stops: the north arcade east pier, paid for by 'maynstrells', depicts five of the town's minstrels in their livery. Both nave and choir have brightly painted flat wooden ceilings with elaborate bosses, the chancel panels painted with English kings.

Off the north transept the late 13th-century Chapel of Holy Trinity, above a vaulted crypt, has a good early 16th-

century ceiling with rich bosses carpentered by W Hall: the c.1335 Chapel of St Michael at the east end of the north aisle has a sensuous tierceron vault. One of the label-stops to the moulded doorway of the vaulted sacristy shows an anthropomorphic rabbit, perhaps the inspiration for the white one encountered by Alice in Wonderland.

The choir stalls, dated 1445, were made by the Ripon school of carvers, some with scurrilous misericords. On the east wall of the south transept is a tablet to Samuel Butler (died 1812), the distinguished actor-manager who built Richmond's Georgian Theatre Royal (see 90, NY), and whose inscription reads: 'A poor Player, that struts and frets his hour upon the Stage, and then is heard no more.' The large black Derbyshire marble font, dated 1530, has an ogee niche carved on each of its eight sides, and inscription band running round the top behind the finials – even the base is enriched.

A route south-east from St Mary's through pleasing Georgian streets and market places comes, by Highgate, to the north transept of Beverley Minster. The north wall of this transept leaned badly until pushed back to verticality in 1716–20 by a timber frame devised by Nicholas Hawksmoor and York carpenter-architect William Thornton, the frame being adjusted by a screw mechanism as the successful operation progressed.

A fine collegiate church, with high quality medieval fittings, and extra east choir transepts, was begun at the east end in the 1220s: the Early English main transepts and first nave bay were up by 1260. When work restarted in 1308 after a break, Gothic architecture had moved on into the Decorated period, and by c.1450, when the graceful twin-towered west front was finished, it was Perpendicular. The result shows remarkable fidelity to the original design, only the large east window of 1410 being obviously an afterthought. The nave vault utilises brick infilling between the stone ribs.

The interior of the minster, even more pleasingly proportioned than the outside, shows more clearly the different dates. The nave, all of creamy stone, its piers with fillets, musicians between the arches, has Decorated wall canopies with fanciful characters, some playing instruments, others apparently contorted with ailments. The large 12th-century black Frosterley marble circular font, on elaborate base, has an immense cover of 1713 grand enough for a London Wren church. In the roof space above the crossing is a 16th-century treadmill for raising heavy materials for maintenance purposes.

The earlier choir and transepts are strongly delineated by black marble shafts and astragals, especially in the triforia: almost colour-matched are dark oak choir stalls of 1520, intricately carved canopies, misericord seats with secular scenes. Hawksmoor's geometric patterned stone floor emphasises the black-and-white theme. The double staircase in the north choir aisle once led up into the chapter house, its Early English trefoil arches on slender black marble shafts with rich stiff-leaf capitals.

In front of the north-east transept, where the Percy Chapel has the chest tomb of Henry Percy (died 1489), is the superb mid-14th-century Percy Tomb. This very Decorated large free-standing canopy – with crocketed gable covering a nodding ogee arch with cusps within cusps, and shield-holding figures in the spandrels – has every inch richly carved with religious scenes, angels, knights,

and foliage. The adjacent octagonal staircase leads up to what was once a loft above the Percy Screen, now forming a reredos. Opposite is a contemporary wooden sedilia, and nearby is an Anglo-Saxon *fridstol* or stone seat, a relic of a church built c.690, on the site of the minster. The earlier church was built by St John of Beverley, who was buried in it, and whose shrine attracted many pilgrims to swell the medieval prosperity of this wool and cloth town.

81
Bradford, W Yorkshire

8 miles (12.8 km) W of Leeds via major roads

Little remains of the old town except Paper Hall, a long-derelict mid-17th-century yeoman's house, saved at last, Bolling Hall, now a museum, and the Perpendicular parish church, now

Cathedral, largely rebuilt. The rest of Bradford is largely splendidly and proudly Victorian, particularly Little Germany, an area of sett-paved steep, narrow streets, flanked by *palazzi*-like warehouses, their beautiful sandstone cleaned, with superbly carved decoration, built by merchants of expensive 'finished' cloth, to attract wealthy home and overseas customers.

Three architectural practices produced these expressions of Bradford's international trading importance: Henry Francis Lockwood and William Mawson, Eli Milnes and Charles France, William Andrews and Joseph Pepper. The classical norm prevailed here, exceptions being the Wool Exchange of 1864–7, with sixteen Corinthian columns beside which million-pound deals were struck, and the Town Hall of 1873, which housed municipal offices, both by Lockwood and Mawson, in Gothic Revival owing more to Italy and France than to England. Many other fine

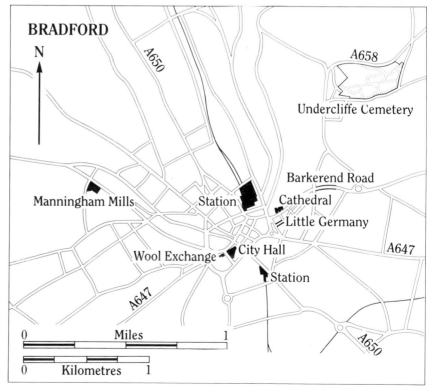

Bradford. EH

Bradford, Undercliffe Cemetery. RCHME

public buildings have been lost.

The smell of wool still pervades Bradford's air, but it is no longer 'Worstedopolis', and many fine mills have either gone or are no longer used for their original purpose. An example is the huge mill built in 1871–3 by Samuel Cunliffe Lister to manufacture silk velvet in Manningham suburb, which it is hoped may become a northern branch of the Victoria & Albert Museum. Andrews' and Pepper's mill consists of two vast five-storey blocks, their elevations almost ¼ mile (0.4 km) long, and an enormous chimney, 262 ft (80 m) high, a prominent feature of the Bradford skyline. Bradford rose to pre-eminence in the later Industrial Revolution because of close proximity to supplies of good coal to power large steam engines, it having been poorly sited for water power. It also had iron ore, and excellent building stone.

The majority of Bradford's Victorian worthies were interred in Undercliffe Cemetery, opened on Otley Road in 1852, a bleak and hilly resting place but carefully planned so that its main east–west axis is on a level. In the centre, two chapels were provided, for Anglicans and Nonconformists. The styles of funerary monument are rich and varied, and the general impression is of black spiky obelisks on the skyline.

82

Coxwold, N Yorkshire

SE 535772. 7 miles (11.2 km) SE of Thirsk, on minor road between A170 Thirsk–Helmsley and A19(T) Thirsk–York roads

An attractive rubble sandstone village, with many important buildings, Coxwold is not formally planned but has grown around crossroads. It is, however, an estate village, attached to Newburgh Priory, once a house of Augustinian canons and now a country house mainly of early 17th- and several 18th-century dates, with good interiors and interesting gardens and ancillary features.

From the crossroads the main street climbs to the west. On the south side are the Fauconberg Almshouses, with central tower porch dated 1662. Higher up is the Church of St Michael, all of c.1430 except for Gothic chancel of 1774 by Thomas Atkinson. The octagonal west tower is particularly distinctive: it seems taller, being at the uphill end, and has narrow angle buttresses, Perpendicular belfry-openings, and pierced parapets between the pinnacles.

The charming interior has nave fittings mostly installed during Laurence Sterne's residency at Shandy Hall in 1760–8. Sterne's original tombstone now stands outside the south nave wall, moved here from Bayswater when that churchyard was cleared for development in 1969. The Perpendicular flat nave roof has painted carved bosses. The altar rail, of good 18th-century turned balusters, is an unusual U-shape to squeeze it between the huge monuments to former owners of Newburgh.

On the north side of the chancel the effigies of William Belasyse (died 1603) and his wife Margaret lie within a large classical entablature with painted strapwork, coats of arms and Latin texts. The tomb is signed by Thomas Browne, with the statement that it is of Hazelwood stone. Next to it Henry Belasyse (died 1647) and his son Thomas, 1st Earl of Fauconberg (died 1700), have life-size white marble figures by John Nost, with putti above bearing the earl's coronet. On the south side, the figures of Thomas, Viscount Fauconberg (died 1632) and his wife Barbara (died 1618) kneel in a large aedicule, and Henry, last Earl Fauconberg (died 1802) and his wife Charlotte (died 1825) have a Gothic chantry-like monument.

Immediately west of the church is Colville Hall, part of a larger early 17th-century manor house. Opposite the church in the Old Hall, really the Grammar School, an inscription records its 1600 foundation by Sir John Hart, Lord Mayor of London, and its links with Sidney (later Sidney Sussex) College, Cambridge. Panelling from the school-room is now in the Porters' Hall at Newburgh Priory. The adjoining master's house was added c.1725. Among the school's pupils was the architect William Wakefield, who came from the nearby village of Huby.

Just west of the village is Shandy Hall, so named by Laurence Sterne who lived here in 1760–8, and in it wrote his

Coxwold. BJAW

A position as far down the Ouse as possible was needed, and the hamlet of Goole was chosen as immediately above the Dutch River formed by early 17th-century Dutch engineer Cornelius Vermuyden.

Creator of the port was the Aire and Calder Navigation Company, and the necessary Act of Parliament was passed in 1820. The original plan by John Rennie was implemented after his death in 1821 by George Leather. As well as the shallow craft used on rivers and canals the docks, first opened in 1826, had to accommodate much larger sea-going vessels with a draught of over 18 ft (5.4 m).

In addition to the engineering works, the Navigation Company had to provide for administration, customs, storage, housing of various standards for the new inhabitants, and suitable quality accommodation for visiting merchants and agents. The first development around Aire Street almost fronted the Ouse, the settlement gradually shifting inland as further docks were built. Little

most famous novel *Tristram Shandy*. A mid-15th-century timber-framed hall house with two gabled two-storey end wings, it was encased in stone and given a new roof of graduated stone slates *c.*1700. A low first floor, reached by a timber staircase in a rear turret, was at the same time inserted into the central hall, but the cross-passage remains. Some 18th-century alterations are known to have been made by Sterne, and the restored building now houses a vast collection of material relating to him.

83

Goole, Humberside

On S side of River Ouse near Humber estuary. Near M62 junction 36

By no stretch of imagination describable as an architectural gem, but of considerable importance in the region's industrial history, Goole was a river port created specifically to transport coal to London from the rich South Yorkshire seams, most 'sea-coal' having hitherto been supplied by Newcastle-upon-Tyne.

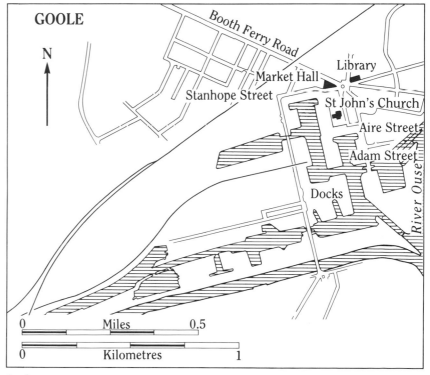

Goole. EH

Goole, hydraulic hoist for lifting 'tom-puddings'. JH

Waterways criss-cross streets in Goole, resulting in a remarkable number of bridges, many designed to open. One narrow foot-bridge was hand-cranked to swing it open. Most machinery on the docks, including lock-gates, was powered by a central hydraulic system, for which there was a hydraulic intensifier in a timber structure. An old dock crane survives, and two examples of a hoist unique to Goole.

William Bartholomew, the Navigation Company's engineer, in 1868 designed a compartment-boat system for the Knottingley–Goole Canal. Rectangular iron barges in uniform trains of nineteen, nick-named 'tom-puddings', were hauled full of coal by steam tugs to Goole, where they were lifted bodily so that the coal tipped into the hold of a collier moored below. The innovation enabled the Aire and Calder Navigation successfully to compete against the railways for the transport of coal far longer than most.

Goole's buildings are generally late

19th-century, mostly in red brick with Welsh slate roofs. In Stanhope Street are the Goods Offices of 1892, and turreted on the corner the contemporary Bank Chambers, in terracotta, now municipal offices. Opposite the new library is the 1896 Market Hall in Art Nouveau style. Nearby on a traffic island, somewhat forlorn, is a classical clock dated 1826, which marks the beginning of Goole.

84
Halifax, W Yorkshire

5 miles (8 km) SW of Bradford on A58

Halifax has an important textile industry history, and was a wool centre in medieval times, when the large Church of St John the Baptist served a huge rural parish. Mostly 15th-century Perpendicular, with lofty nave arcades, double south aisle, long chancel with clerestory, the west tower is constructed on higher ground. Interesting interior

survives from the early years, but one of the oldest buildings is the Lowther Hotel, a three-storey seven-bay building in dark-brown brick, generally Georgian in character. Nearby in Aire Street is a terrace of three-storey houses, including the Royal Hotel, behind which the former 'Public Rooms' and theatre share an arcaded elevation.

The original terraces had distinctive rounded corners. Because the land was low-lying, the roads were made up to a level above their lowest storey. Two-storey houses in Adam Street (which was demolished in 1973) had brick-vaulted basement kitchens, level with rear yards containing outside lavatories, coal-houses and wash-houses; living rooms had stone floors and tiled fireplaces; above were two bedrooms; two more in the loft had ladder access.

The Perpendicular-style 1843 Church of St John, cruciform in plan with a spire, is a credit to the Navigation Company. More of a landmark from the surrounding flat countryside is the tall narrow brick water-tower of 1883, the supports buttressed, the tank with domical roof; next to it stands its larger reinforced concrete successor of 1926.

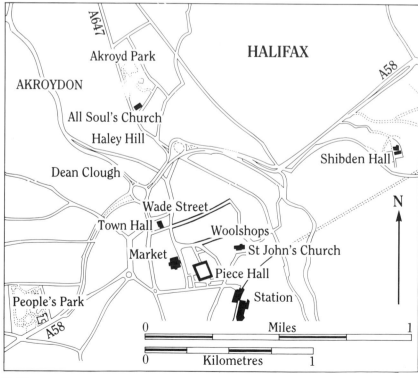

Halifax. EH

Halifax skyline. ES

features include flat ceilings of 1636, with painted panels in the chancel, 15th-century font cover, Jacobean box-pews and chests, fine altar rail, and near the south door a particularly appealing poor box – a life-size figure carved as a beggar-man, known as Old Tristram. The external flagging, as in many West Riding churches, consists of re-used well-lettered tombstones.

Prosperous local clothiers built many fine yeoman houses. Shibden Hall, now a museum, is in core a timber-framed H-plan early 15th-century house; 16th-century alterations included a segmental-arched kitchen fireplace with ogee-section chamfer. Largely faced in stone in the 17th century, the central house-body front wall was brought forward, with a very large window with ovolo-section transoms and mullions: some of its old glass quarries were painted by Baernard Dinninckhoff of York. A first floor was inserted into the house-body, and some upstairs fireplaces are Tudor-arched, with tridents and tulips in the spandrels. There is 16th- and 17th-century panelling, some of it inlaid, some with Ionic frieze. Early 19th-century alterations included adding the tall and rather ugly tower.

Cloth merchants in many West Riding towns banded together in the late 18th century to erect cloth halls where cloth makers could gather to market their goods for the greater convenience of the prosperous merchants. Most cloth halls have gone, but that at Halifax survives intact, known as the Piece Hall, because a piece was an understood measure of cloth. Vast and very impressive, it is a monument to hand-powered cloth manufacture which, in 1779 when it opened, was about to be replaced by water-powered machines.

The honey-coloured sandstone building had over three hundred merchants' rooms on two and three galleries around a large sloping quadrangle. To provide security for the valuable cloth, the outside walls are blind, except for gateways central in each side, and gallery access is only from inside, with corner staircases. The ground-floor gallery is fronted with an arcade, the first floor with rusticated piers, the second with Tuscan columns.

Nonconformity was strong: the Congregationalists built Square Chapel in 1772, a five-bay classical building with pediment and central Venetian window, in brick – rare in Halifax. After many years' sore neglect it is being restored as an arts centre. Next to it a tall Decorated-style spire is all that survives of its successor church of 1855.

In Wade Street, facades of the Zion Chapel of 1819, also Congregational and also long-threatened – its rather severe Greek Revival Doric portico with slightly projecting side wings and attic storey, and adjoining 1846 Sunday School with round-arched windows between Tuscan pilasters and square campanile – have been successfully incorporated into a bus station with a Modernist black and green metal and glass structure.

New life has also been breathed into the huge Dean Clough Mill complex, once a carpet factory employing 6,000, now home to many young enterprises. It was built in 1842–57 by John Crossley, whose family played a dominant part in the cultural, political and religious life of Halifax. Sir Francis Crossley gave to the town the People's Park, laid out by Sir Joseph Paxton in 1856.

Another prominent family, the Akroyds, built two model mill villages, Copley and Akroydon. Edward Akroyd bought Copley worsted spinning mill in 1844, but found it too far away for the additional work-force he hoped to recruit to walk from existing settlements. Copley village, begun in 1849, and probably designed by William Henry Crossland who worked for George Gilbert Scott, has been left without a focus since the fine mill was demolished.

Akroydon, begun in 1859 by George Gilbert Scott himself in 'domestic Gothic' style, more lavish in layout with better houses and open spaces, was funded by a pioneering partnership with the Halifax Permanent Benefit Building Society. The houses were not rented from Akroyd, but purchased through low-interest mortgages which he guaranteed.

Edward Akroyd's mansion, Bankfield, is on Haley Hill, where in 1856–9 he built the magnificent Church of All Souls, described by Scott as 'on the

whole, my best church', its crocketed tower with tall spire a landmark from Halifax itself, although the limestone has severely decayed. Polished marbles and granites, mosaics and stained glass give a very rich interior.

During his mayoralty of 1850–1, John Crossley planned civic buildings worthy of Halifax's manufacturing importance, submitting an Italianate Lockwood and Mawson design for a Town Hall. Edward Akroyd countered with a Gothic Scott design. A 'Battle of the Styles', and of local interests, lasted several years, but had a successful outcome, in that in 1859 Sir Charles Barry designed a suitably dominant and very grand tall-spired Town Hall. Halifax has retained its Victorian covered Borough Market of 1895, and several nearby Victorian streets are now carefully conserved and cherished. Even the modern shopping centre, the Woolshops, is better than many. A former railway shed has become a Museum for Children, called 'Eureka!'

85

Harrogate, N Yorkshire

13 miles (20.9 km) NE of Leeds via A61

A hilly spa town, characterised by vast green open spaces, Harrogate is always a credit to municipal gardeners' skills. The sulphur and iron springs are down in the Valley Gardens, the latter created in 1887 to commemorate Queen Victoria's Golden Jubilee. By the late 18th century Harrogate was a popular meeting place for northern society, particularly the intelligentsia who gathered in the hotels for conversation as much as spa water.

The Crown Hotel was one of the earliest: its pilastered main block typically rather sombre, Harrogate always being extremely decorous, though the 1870 additions are slightly more ostentatious. The Royal Baths, opened in 1897, with Italianate *porte-cochère*, still offer coffee-morning concerts in the Assembly Room, with its dome high above paired Corinthian marbled columns, and health-inducing texts on the frieze. Art Nouveau stained glass fills what are technically, intentionally or not, thermal windows. The Parliament Room, for smaller assemblies, has panelled walls and vaulted ceiling. The Lounge Hall beyond of *c.*1930 is Art Deco, its courtyard with fountain, the surrounding glazed roofing on Tuscan colonnade. Spa treatments are, sadly, not available but there are Turkish baths and a sauna suite.

The Royal Pump Room, now Harrogate Museum, was designed in 1842 with a hint of Grecian influence by Isaac Thomas Shutt of the Swan Hotel, with ogee dome and open cupola of cast-ironwork. In the early 19th century Betty Lupton, the 'Queen of the Wells', dispensed the waters, but now there is

Harrogate, Royal Baths. HARROGATE RESORT SERVICES

just a public drinking fountain. The Pump Room Annexe of 1913, in cast iron and glass, has a lead roof worked in elaborate lozenge-tile pattern.

The Duchy of Lancaster only began to develop Harrogate on a larger scale in 1840, and several stone terraces are from this date, many originally of boarding houses, now often hotels. Several older parades of shops are now antique shops; later ones, like Montpellier Parade, have curved glass display windows, a few still with Art Nouveau panels above. Some cast-iron canopies remain, notably on Betty's famous tea shop facing Prospect Square.

86
Heath, W Yorkshire

SE 355200. 1 mile (1.6 km) SE of Wakefield, N of A655

Within sight of Wakefield, under the shadow of two power-station cooling towers, the village is surprisingly fine, its millstone grit houses spread around the edge of Heath Common, like an unusually large village green. To add to the amazement, several of the houses are unexpectedly grand.

Robert Smythson's Old Hall of c.1585 has sadly been lost, but next to its site is Heath House, by the young James Paine, begun in 1744. Also, further east is Heath Hall, rebuilt c.1754 by John Carr, his first country house and one of his

best. With central pediment on giant Ionic columns, it already has the canted bay windows which are such a feature of his designs.

The interiors of Heath Hall have fine wood-carving, and exquisite rococo plasterwork probably by the elder Joseph Rose, particularly in the drawing room, where walls are treated as if comprised of Ionic Venetian windows, with beautiful flowing scrolls and leaves above, as well as on the ceiling. The external composition includes very grand flanking pavilions, stable block to left, service range to right, these with tall cupolas, very large central arches, and pediments to both main and subsidiary elevations.

Such mansions needed plenty of water, and the village was served by an 18th-century water-tower. An area as prosperous as this was also likely to generate some above-average monuments, and the parish church at nearby Kirkthorpe has several, but the area necessitates its being kept locked.

87
Hull, Humberside

On N side of Humber estuary, 4 miles (6.4 km) NE of Humber Bridge

Kingston upon Hull, commonly referred to as Hull, got its name when acquired by Edward I in 1293. The old harbour

was on the River Hull which joins the Humber just east of the High Street, where the merchants lived, and their wharves lay between the river and the street. On the edge of the Hull by Drypool Bridge, now converted into housing, are timber-framed warehouses, unusually large for their 1745 and 1760 dates, built by Joseph Pease, Hull's first banker and early industrial entrepreneur.

North of the High Street are the former Dock Offices of c.1820, with Roman Doric portico, pediment with clock, and cupola above. No. 6 High Street, called Blaydes House after 18th-century merchant Benjamin Blaydes, a three-storey, five-bay house in small bricks, with Roman Doric portico, was partially rebuilt c.1760 with good staircase. Nos 23 and 24 High Street, a six-bay pair of three-storey 1750s houses – with Ionic-columned door-cases and sash windows with tripartite-keystoned brick flat arches – now form part of the adjacent museum wherein was born slavery abolitionist William Wilberforce in 1759.

Wilberforce House, rebuilt c.1660 on the site of a house where merchant John Lister entertained Charles I in 1642, in 1709 passed to cloth and lead exporter John Thornton. The latter took as apprentice one William Wilberforce, who in 1711 married Thornton's daughter Sarah, and made a fortune in Baltic trade. William and Sarah took over in 1732, replaced brick-mullioned windows with larger sashes, extending the house to rear in a plan needing light-wells, because the land was hemmed in by wharf buildings. Their son Robert and his wife Elizabeth altered the house c.1760, just after son William was born.

The new staircase, necessitated by the erection of the adjoining pair of houses blocking the original staircase window, is exceedingly fine: its curly hand-rail (a Hull feature) carried by richly-carved baluster columns on a variety of urns; the stair undersides panelled. The Venetian window surround has exquisite plasterwork, with a delectable vine growing above. The splendid ceiling has a central black eagle – the family crest – and four

Heath Hall. WAKEFIELD MDC

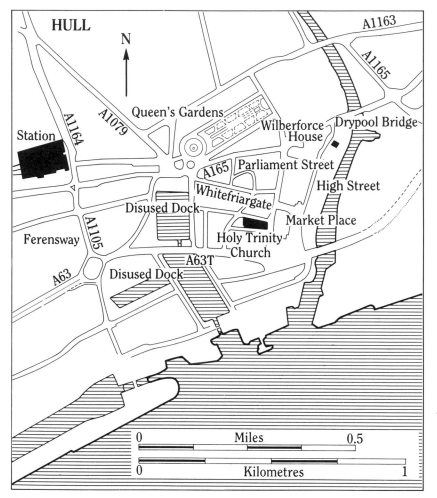

HULL

Queen's Gardens

Wilberforce House

Drypool Bridge

Station

Parliament Street

High Street

Whitefriargate

Disused Dock

Market Place

Ferensway

Holy Trinity Church

Disused Dock

A1163
A1165
A1164
A1079
A1165
A1105
A63
A63T

| 0 | Miles | 0.5 |
| 0 | Kilometres | 1 |

Hull. EH

Maisters House (NT), five bays, three storeys plus basement, is in plain brickwork except for the stone sill band to the first-floor sash windows, and even the Ionic pedimented door-case is extremely restrained. This serves to add great drama to the splendours inside. The pine-panelled counting-house rooms are solidly sober: the access to the family's upper floors is not.

The open-well cantilevered stone staircase, top-lit from octagonal dome, has wrought-iron balustrades by Robert Bakewell of Derby. Acanthus roses in square panels adorn the first-floor landing soffit, rococo ribboning the second. Staircase hall and upper landings doors have six fielded panels, each door-case with acanthus-leaf pulvinated frieze and Ionic cornice. The staircase walls have dado panelling, swept at the corners, with Vitruvian scrolls on the landing; statue niches and picture panels below cloth-and-shell drops – the plasterwork is by John Page of Hull. The principal reception room was refitted, with pretty chimney-piece, when the younger Henry married Margaret Pennyman in 1760. Behind No. 41 High Street another 'Artisan Mannerist' tower porch with jewelled pilasters like Wilberforce House, is dated 1664 and has the initials *GC* and *EC* of merchant George Crowle and wife.

Merchants' private staithes were replaced from the late 18th century by a number of docks. After many years' dereliction, and some back-filling, the last decade has seen regeneration. Railway Dock and Humber Dock are now Hull Marina, opened 1983, with new housing and hotel and a permanently moored Spurn lightship. Prince's Quay is now a waterside shopping centre.

To its east in the old Market Place is Holy Trinity Church, said to be the largest English parish church in floor area. Of cruciform plan, with large Perpendicular central tower of *c.*1500, and eight-bay nave of *c.*1400, its Decorated early 14th-century chancel and transepts are in exceptionally early brick. The large east window is now reflected in the Midland Bank's bronzed glass. Nearby, with mullioned-and-transomed brick windows, the Old Grammar School, founded in 1583, is

corner busts. The same plasterer probably did the dining room rococo ceiling.

Hull merchants usually put the ground floors of their houses to counting-house and other business use, and so the family living rooms of Wilberforce House are a storey up. Two first-floor front rooms have 17th-century panelling, the banqueting room also has an elaborate chimney-piece with fretwork frieze, the bedroom a Dutch-tiled fireplace. The 'Artisan Mannerist' exterior has a tower porch with brick Corinthian pilasters, broken into bands, each with a raised stone lozenge. The house is set back from the High Street behind a low brick wall with

tall brick gate-piers, similarly rusticated.

After the Hull Transport Museum comes the Hull and East Riding Museum in the ashlar Corn Exchange of 1856, with large Corinthian columns. Opposite is the house of the Baltic-trading Maister family, who held public office in Hull. In April 1743 their old house caught fire, and the then Mrs Henry Maister, her infant daughter and two servants perished. Her husband Henry began rebuilding straight away but died the following year, so work was carried on for his son (also Henry) and was supervised by elder Henry's brother Nathaniel, who involved in the design Lord Burlington, owner of an East Riding estate.

where Puritan poet and MP for Hull, Andrew Marvell, was a pupil, as well as William Wilberforce. Until 1706 the Merchant Adventurers of Hull shared the building with the school.

To the north is Trinity House, its impressive 1753 frontage block of two low storeys, 3:3:3 bays, the centre with segmental-pedimented Tuscan door-case, and pediment with royal coat of arms flanked by reclining figures Neptune and Britannia. The school has broken with tradition to admit girls.

In Whitefriargate the former Neptune Inn (1794–7), with its central segmental arch for coaches, was a very grand composition of 3:1:5:1:3 bays, the first floor, once the Assembly Room, with tripartite and Venetian windows, and panels of urns. A nearby building of 3:5:3 bays has Ionic columns and pedimented first-floor windows, a central pediment with gross figures.

Parliament Street is a unified Georgian development of c.1800. To the east on the corner of Silver Street and Lowgate is Hepworth's Arcade of 1894, with curved glass roof. Further north are Queen's Gardens, formerly the Queen's Dock of 1775, the earliest of the docks. At one end on a Greek Doric

column is a statue of Wilberforce; at the other end Queen Victoria Square, with imposing civic buildings. Nearby is the recently excavated site of Beverley Gate, where the English Civil War started in 1642, when Parliamentarian Hull under its Governor Sir John Hotham refused to admit Charles I.

Across Ferensway, if potential rail passengers ever get across, is Paragon Street Station. The fine Italianate hotel of 2:2:5:2:2 sandstone ashlar bays, three storeys plus attic, and overhanging cornice on brackets, has been restored after suffering a dreadful fire late in 1990. The 1846 station by G T Andrews stands behind a poor modern extension. The good concourse has dark green round arches and ribs, cream wooden panels, tiles and faience, and Art Nouveau lavatories.

88

Leeds, W Yorkshire

8 miles (12.8 km) E of Bradford via major roads

This brief description of Leeds is mainly chronological, as the city is too large to

describe coherently in any geographical order. The pre-Conquest settlement lay around the parish church of St Peter, in which is an Anglo-Scandinavian cross, its tapering shaft carved with recessed panels, one showing Weland, the flying smith. The church was rebuilt in 1837–41 by Robert Dennis Chantrell, who had moved to Leeds in 1819 after being a pupil of Sir John Soane. The galleried interior reflects the theological views of Dr Walter Farquhar Hook, who became Vicar of Leeds in 1837, and introduced the robed choir which became ubiquitous in 19th-century English churches.

In 1207 Briggate was laid out as a wide market place flanked by sixty equal burgage plots. The plan is still traceable today, the large shops occupying two or three such plots. In Lambert's Yard off Lower Briggate one timber-framed building remains, recently refurbished, a 17th-century late example.

A long and distinguished industrial history owes much to the Cistercian Kirkstall Abbey, 3 miles (4.8 km) from medieval Leeds in the country. The town grew in the 17th century, and expanded north to New Briggate, where St John's Church was built in 1631–4 by John Harrison, a generous philanthropist and one of the wealthy woollen merchants who successfully petitioned Charles I for the charter granting Leeds borough status in 1626. The exterior is a rare example of Gothic Survival; the unusual interior, with nave and south aisle of equal width and richly carved wooden fittings, reflects the anti-Puritan influence of Archbishop William Laud.

In 1722 Lady Elizabeth Hastings, a woman of great drive and a generous patroness of building projects, encouraged the prospering merchants of Leeds to build themselves the suitably grand church of Holy Trinity in Boar Lane. The architect was William Etty of York, although it has often been attributed to William Halfpenny, who in 1725 published a drawing of similar Wren-like design. Etty himself probably carved the sanctuary woodwork.

The merchants' wealth was, of course, generated by woollen cloth. In Crown Street is the entrance, with pediment and cupola, of the White Cloth

Hull, the docks in the 1960s. DIS

95

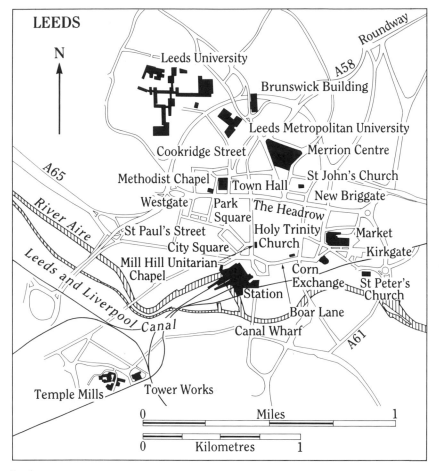

Leeds. EH

podium of steps and passes between tall columns, to domed foyer with Corinthian pilasters, anthemion floor tiles, statues of the Queen dated 1858, and of Prince Consort dated 1865. Inside are three courts and tile-lined staircases. The main auditorium is the Victoria Hall, splendid with pairs of pink Corinthian columns, on tall plinths of vividly coloured marbles, and with an ornate barrel roof. In the far apse a marvellously proud organ is set high above steeply raked seating tiers for large choirs, with orchestra below.

Behind the Town Hall is Sir George Gilbert Scott's Infirmary of 1863–7, and to the north up Cookridge Street the Institute, now Civic Theatre, and terraced Gothic shops, both by Brodrick. To the east are George Corson's Italianate Municipal Buildings of 1884, now library and museum, the grandiose staircase with fine decorative wall-tiles, made locally in Burmantofts.

Brodrick was also responsible for the second finest Victorian building in Leeds, the 1861–3 Corn Exchange, now imaginatively converted into shops. Externally a stunning ellipse of rusticated stonework, with two stages of round-arched windows and curving Tuscan portico: internally each corn merchant's office had a numbered round-arched doorway, those on the upper tier accessed from a cast-iron fronted balcony.

Another fine Victorian public building is George Corson's Grand Theatre in New Briggate, opened in 1878, with truly grand and many-tiered auditorium. In the same year St Paul's House was built as a large factory and warehouse for Sir John Barran, pioneer of the ready-made clothing for which Leeds became famous. Designed by Thomas Ambler in Hispano-Moorish style, it is built of brick with terracotta decorative details; the distinctive skyline minarets at the canted corners and pierced gableted parapets are now fibreglass replacements.

There are other exciting buildings inspired by foreign sources, notably a flax mill, Temple Mills, Marshall Street, Holbeck, modelled on Egyptian temples at Edfu. Built in the 1830s, the mill was designed by noted Egyptologist Joseph

Hall of 1775. The Assembly Rooms form one side of the former courtyard plan, with their round-arched ground-floor openings, and first-floor thermal windows with central pedimented feature containing a Venetian window.

Successful 18th-century inhabitants built fine houses on the outskirts – Kirkstall Grange, perhaps by James Paine, and Gledhow Hall, probably by John Carr – and just west of the centre, more modest in scale, Park Square of the 1760s, still a relative oasis with central gardens, York-stone pavements, and cast-iron railings to the houses. A Georgian building in the industrial heart is the Leeds and Liverpool Canal Company warehouse, built in 1777 at the basin where the then-as-yet-incomplete canal met the older Aire Navigation.

Leeds has memorably grand 19th-century buildings although many have been lost, and the Victorian Society has had to fight extremely hard to save others. The city's most monumental building is the Town Hall designed by Cuthbert Brodrick and famously opened by Queen Victoria in 1858: huge, surrounded by enormous Corinthian columns and pilasters, skilfully modelled with projecting corner and parapet details with balustrades and urns. The immensely successful tower – a dome with clock and booming bell pushed skyward by a square colonnade on an enriched stage – was an afterthought.

Surely daunting, even to the Empress of India, is the entry to this building – the visitor mounts the huge

Leeds, Briggate *c*.1890. MANSELL COLLECTION

Bonomi in consultation with Leeds engineer James Combe, and was, in addition to its revivalistic elevations, also very advanced technically. In nearby Globe Road are two fragments of Tower Works: local architect Thomas Shaw's 1864 factory chimney copying the Lamberti tower, Verona, and Leeds architect William Bakewell's 1899 dust-extraction chimney, a brown brick and Burmantofts faience copy of Giotto's white marble Florentine campanile.

Briggate's narrow burgage plots led to the development of the covered shopping arcades. First came Thornton's Arcade, built in 1878 for publican Charles Thornton who owned the City Varieties Theatre. In Gothic style, it seems narrow, as the buildings are three storeys high; the glazed roof has horseshoe-shaped cast-iron arches; the decoration includes portrait heads, and at one end is a clock with mechanical figures from Scott's *Ivanhoe*.

Queen's Arcade of 1888, slightly wider and of only two storeys, has an upper tier of shops with a sinuously curved cast-iron access balcony. The County Arcade of 1898 was designed by theatre architect Frank Matcham, with terracotta external elevations, faience inside, and shops with bold Ionic columns. The round-arched roof trusses have been picked out in cream and green during restoration as part of what is now called the Victoria Quarter which has involved the roofing-over of the adjoining Queen Victoria Street, also developed by the Leeds Estates Company. Tall columns support the new roof, with cheerful psychedelic-colour panels which also cast detracting shadows on the rich Edwardian decoration.

Across The Headrow – mid-20th-century town planning good in scale but poor in individual design – is the Grand Arcade of 1898: architecturally less interesting, though planned as a double avenue of shops, it has an entertaining clock, with figures of knights in armour, a guardsman, Scotsman, Irishman, Canadian and Indian.

On the corner of Kirkgate and Vicar Lane are the City Markets, rebuilt in 1903–4 to a design by Leeming and Leeming of Halifax, the cast-iron interior planned around a central octagon – originally with the clock now at Oakwood. The basilican St Aidan's Church in Roundhay Road (1891–4), by R J Johnson and A Crawford-Hick, has Ravenna-like mosaics by Sir Frank Brangwyn. The famous Quarry Hill 1930s housing came to the end of its structural life and was demolished, but of the period is W Curtis Green's Portland stone Queen's Hotel for the London, Midland and Scottish Railway.

In City Square Alfred Drury's electric-torch-bearing Art Nouveau statues now merely decorate a large roundabout: behind them Henry Tanner's 1896 Italianate General Post Office was cleaned except for its clock tower. Nearby Unitarian Mill Hill Chapel of 1848 (so called because the Presbyterian congregation established in 1672 was on Mill Hill) is by Manchester's Bowman and Crowther, and the Perpendicular-style cruciform plan has a surprisingly Anglican interior. It is most famous for having had as its minister in 1767–73 Joseph Priestley, who discovered oxygen.

Leeds has taken particular pride in educational establishments. The core of the University is by Alfred Waterhouse: 1920s and 1930s additions in Portland stone included the clock tower which features on the skyline. Leeds Metropolitan University (formerly Leeds Polytechnic) has made one major contribution to architectural history, the 1975 Brunswick Building – one of the last 'Modern' buildings before the vogue turned to Post-modernism. Intended to enclose on three sides a space with a sense of place, only two-thirds were built, and completion is now unlikely. Designed by the City Architect's department, its composition is a tribute to the determination of the then Director of the Polytechnic, Dr Patrick Nuttgens, an architect and architectural critic.

89
New Earswick, N Yorkshire

SE 609553. 2 miles (3.2 km) N of York on York–Haxby road

The third English 'garden' settlement, after Port Sunlight and Bournville, New Earswick was created by the Joseph Rowntree Village Trust, not directly by the Rowntree chocolate firm, with which it was nevertheless closely associated. The architect was Raymond Unwin, nationally famous for the almost-contemporary Letchworth, the first garden city.

New Earswick was not a suburb to an older settlement, but an entirely new village, just north of York, straddling the

New Earswick. RCHME

York–Haxby road. On its west side is the Folk Hall, whitewashed roughcast walls below large steep red pantile roof. Built as an institute, the library is next door, and attached to its other end, significantly, is the Quaker Meeting House. The village garage is beyond, but in New Earswick the car is kept in its rightful subordinate place. The village is pedestrian-orientated, and cars are restricted to secondary routes, with limited access in some areas. Further north is the original village school.

Between the east side of the road and the small River Foss are the original houses, mostly in short, visually self-contained terraces. Opposite the Folk Hall the straight Station Avenue no longer leads to a station, but the other streets meander. Now the planting is mature, the leafy effect lives up to the addresses: to the south, Poplar Grove with small picturesque green-flanked beck; to the north, Chestnut Grove and Sycamore Avenue.

Some of the Arts and Crafts Movement flavour has been lost by removal of chimneys from most houses, done innocently with Utopian intentions when gas central heating was installed. Otherwise the effect faithfully reflects the founders' ideals, to create high standard housing for working people, and from it to generate enough return on capital to fund maintenance etc.

Still owned by the Rowntree Village Trust, the houses are still rented, no alterations reflect the 'Right to Buy', and no 'gentrification' penetrates the egalitarian concept. Everywhere is the commitment to William Morris ideals –

allotments full of vegetables, well-tended gardens with greenhouses, pet rabbits in hutches, and washing lines, many indicating child occupants. A network of footpaths crosses between the houses, some even flanked by high hedges, which would be menacing on many housing estates, but here even the teenagers who cannot resist the temptation to cycle through them seem to do so considerately.

90
Richmond, N Yorkshire

4 miles (6.4 km) SW of Scotch Corner on A6108 and 3 miles (4.8 km) W of A1

The medieval town grew up adjoining the fine Norman castle (see 51, NY), on a hilly site far better for defence than settlement – even the large Market Place is on a pronounced slope. The town was walled c.1311 due to increasing hostility with Scotland just before the Battle of Bannockburn: two postern gates survive, in narrow streets called The Bar and Friars Wynd, the latter constructed to allow the inhabitants to obtain good drinking water from the house of the Grey Friars just outside the town. The Franciscans came in 1258, their buildings lowly until c.1500, when they inserted a fine belfry tower between their nave and choir. The slender Grey Friars Tower, with delicate Perpendicular decoration, is Richmond's most attractive medieval building, looking even loftier without attached buildings.

In the Market Place, originally the castle outer bailey, Trinity Chapel is now the Regimental Museum of the Green Howards. St Mary's parish church in Frenchgate, the oldest suburb, was largely rebuilt by Sir George Gilbert Scott, but the fine tower is of c.1400. Inside are choir stalls from Easby Abbey (17, NY), only just pre-Reformation, and interesting monuments include Robert Smythson's to Timothy Hutton (died 1629). Of three medieval chapels on radial roads, the early 17th-century Bowes Hospital on Anchorage Hill re-uses the 12th-century Chapel of St Edmund King and Martyr.

Richmond prospered as the market town of Swaledale – an area where lead was mined extensively, and wool was knitted into caps and stockings – and its function as an important commercial centre resulted in its predominantly Georgian townscape. Few houses have individual architectural merit, but dramatic topography gives a pleasing overall effect. The two best Georgian streets differ in effect though both are wide and cobbled, for Newbiggin is straight and level, Frenchgate steep and curving.

Its picturesque medieval ruins and scenic topography contributed to the town's 18th-century rise as a major provincial social centre. Town houses were built by many local gentry families, such as the Bathursts, owners of Arkengarthdale lead-mines, whose large early 18th-century Market Place house, and rear pleasure garden with bowling green and cockpit, became the King's Head Hotel, one of several hostelries

Richmond from the Terrace. EH

which played an important part in providing facilities for those participating in the social 'season'.

In 1746, one of Richmond's two Members of Parliament, John Yorke, and his wife with the Hanoverian name Anne, built a temple to celebrate the

Duke of Cumberland's victory over the Stuarts, for Whigs would have been bereft if the Jacobites had won. The Gothick tower, more belvedere than folly, has two good rooms from which there are fine views of the town and surrounding woods and hills: as it is also an important landmark in the Richmond scenery, it is appropriate that the so-called Culloden Tower is now a Landmark Trust property.

Despite the town's Whig sympathies, one resident was Roger Strickland, whose Jacobite younger brother Francis, a close companion of Charles Edward Stuart, took part in the 1715 Rebellion, and was the only Englishman among the 'Seven Men of Moidart' who landed with the 'Bonny Prince' in 1745. Roger Strickland's home in 1727–49 was Oglethorpe House, a Georgianised early 17th-century house in Pottergate. Nearby, hidden by trees, is Hill House, a Georgianised late 16th-century house which, in the mid-18th century, was the home of the grandparents of Frances I'Anson, whose husband Leonard MacNally wrote for her the famous song 'Sweet Lass of Richmond Hill'.

Foremost among the Georgian 'society' entertainments was the 'assembly', a formal ball under a Master of Ceremonies' chairmanship, with card parties and light refreshments. The 1756 purpose-built assembly room is a gracious first-floor ballroom entered by an imperial staircase. It is now the Town Hall, and has an early 18th-century magistrates' court, with fittings

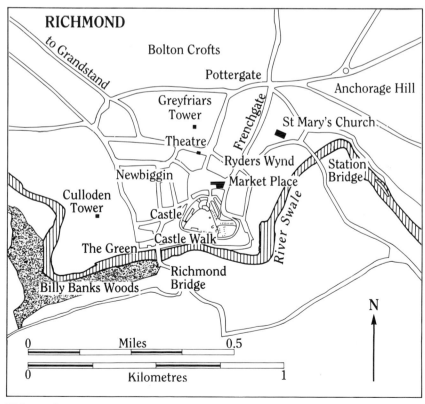

Richmond. EH

including a royal coat of arms, dated 1732, surrounded by the town's thirteen medieval trade guilds' arms. Hanging in the Council Chamber is an original portrait of Queen Elizabeth I, whose 1576 charter gave Richmond two Members of Parliament.

The social season centred on September races. Horses were raced here from Elizabethan times, but a new course was laid out in 1765 and a grandstand designed by John Carr of York was built in 1775 by public subscription. Racing ceased in 1891, but part of the grandstand remains, and may even be restored. The judge's box of 1814 survives intact. Richmond races were on a par with those of York and Doncaster, and in their heyday the prize for the premier Gold Cup race was a silver-gilt trophy designed by Robert Adam.

A remarkable survival from fashionable Georgian times is the Theatre Royal, built in 1788 by actor-manager Samuel Butler (see 80, H) and restored in 1962. It retains its original form, with pit, boxes and gallery, even to the pay-box beside the door from Friars Wynd – there is no proscenium arch, entry to the steeply raked deep stage being by side doors. Excellent acoustics are due to the auditorium proportions, encouraging dialogue between actors and audience, for drama then had political as much as entertainment intent.

A cheaper Georgian social activity was promenading, dressing up and going out to see others, and to be seen by them. For this, scenic walks were laid out in Billy Banks Woods, Easby Woods and the Castle Walk, providing spectacular views down to the Swale. The topography giving these lovely views made, and makes, traffic circulation difficult. A marked increase in the number of Georgian carriages was a parallel to the post-war growth of the motor car. Familiar-sounding measures were implemented to tackle the problem: medieval gateways were demolished, and new streets formed. A narrow medieval bridge was replaced in 1788 by the present Green or Richmond Bridge, a fine and graceful structure designed by the North Riding bridge-

master, the architect John Carr of York. The growing town's water supply was improved in 1771 when the medieval market cross was replaced by a tall obelisk, set above a reservoir, which stored water from springs outside the town, and gravity-fed water points.

The railway further altered traffic circulation in 1846. It was topographically impossible to bring it into the hilly town itself, and the terminus was sited just across the River Swale, linked by a bridge. The line from Darlington was one of George Hudson's, and his architect was George Townsend Andrews of York. The stations along it were in 'Jacobethan' style, that at Richmond having a five-bay Gothic *porte-cochère*, and interior cast-ironwork by Walker of York with Gothick motifs in the spandrels of Tudor arches. The goods station was successfully and usefully replaced in 1974 by a swimming bath designed by the Napper Errington Collerton Partnership.

91
Ripley, N Yorkshire

SE 285605. 3½ miles (5.6 km) N of Harrogate on A61

This estate is a recommendation for late 20th-century hereditary ownership, being a thriving concern, with quality shops so good that people come here from outside for their wares. There are no garish chain-store fascias here, for all are of individual character, and make good use of village buildings, even the front rooms of houses, as in times past.

The attractive planned village, although uniform in scale and materials, has a variety of house sizes, from terraced cottages to small villas. Some are traditionally Georgian, but most are in the Gothick style characteristic of Sir William Amcotts Ingilby's 1820s remodelling, inspired by villages in Alsace-Lorraine. At the north end is the 'Hôtel de Ville' – Town Hall – dated 1854; opposite, and set back, is the former school, which was built in 1702 and rebuilt in 1830, a pretty little box with lattice-paned Gothick windows and

Ripley Castle. DIS

a pyramidal roof. The cobbled Market Place has a cross, on steps.

Inside the much-cherished Church of All Saints, its west tower with large stair turret, are many Ingilby monuments, including that of Sir Thomas, Judge of Assize in 1361, who died in 1369, his recumbent effigy as a knight in chain-mail lying beside his wife on a chest below a nodding ogee-arched niche in the south aisle. Nearby is part of an old rood screen, also with ogee-headed openings, and robust tracery; in the floor below a medieval priest's grave cover. On the south side of the chancel is the grand monument of Sir William Ingilby (died 1618). The chancel has a double piscina.

The hub of the village is Ripley Castle, a fortified manor house owned by the Ingilby family for 670 years. The oldest part is the 15th-century gatehouse. The house has a mid-16th-century peel-tower, complete with priest-hole, but the rest is of the 1780s, battlemented externally but wholly classical inside, almost rococo in elegance. The cantilevered stone staircase, a half-ellipse in plan, has a Venetian landing window with heraldic glass by William Peckitt. The house has a fine parkland setting, with lake, and early 19th-century gardens with orangery and greenhouses.

92

Saltburn-by-the-Sea, Cleveland

NZ 666213. 15 miles (24.1 km) NW of Whitby

To a staid adult, Saltburn is the acceptable face of the seaside: a pretty, sandy bay set below cliffs, on top of which are terraces of houses, several named after jewels – Diamond, Emerald, Ruby, Garnet, etc. The promontory just to the east of the town, Hunt Cliff, housed a Roman signal station, and gave its name to a type of coarse Roman pottery. Before the mid-19th century Saltburn was a hamlet known mostly for smuggling, and plundering the many wrecks which the treacherous sea brought to its beach, and the Ship Inn dates back to these times.

Modern Saltburn was created by Quaker Henry Pease, Member of Parliament for South Durham, and Stockton and Darlington Railway Company board member, who realised that railway profits from transporting ironstone to Middlesbrough could be augmented by passenger traffic if respectable seaside recreation were created within convenient reach of Teesside's expanding population.

Pease first established the Saltburn Improvement Company, which acquired land from the Earl of Zetland of nearby Marske-by-the-Sea. Development began in 1861. At first buildings were of light-coloured firebrick produced by Pease's Darlington Iron Company; later, hard red Accrington brick was used with terracotta, cast iron for sea-facing balconies and shop canopies.

In 1863 Lord Zetland opened the fifty-bedroom Zetland Hotel. Italianate in cream brick with balconies, designed by William Peachey of Darlington, the railway company's architect, it was considered one of the finest railway hotels in the world. Direct covered access from the station was provided by a glass canopy over a special platform; this has gone, and the Zetland is now luxury flats.

The truncated pier, now one of relatively few surviving, was originally almost 1,500 ft long. When it opened in 1869, visitors paid at twin entrance boxes with small roof spires, they could patronise mid-way refreshment booths, and either sit in the pier-end saloon, or descend to the landing stage for a pleasure-steamer trip. Throughout its history the pier has suffered gale and tide damage, and in 1924 was breached by the storm-wrecked *Ovenbeg*. Very high tides in 1953 and 1973 caused severe damage, and in 1974 a violent gale tore away the pier-end near the *Ovenbeg* repair.

The Cliff Lift was built near the pier in 1884 to link Marine Parade and Lower Promenade. The inclined tramway has two cars, with stained glass windows and red plush upholstery, which take 20 seconds to travel up or down the cliff face. Behind each is a water tank: the lower car's tank is emptied, the upper's filled to be heavier, and as it descends the upper car hauls up the lighter lower car with its passengers.

The quiet glen where Skelton Beck meets the sea was landscaped into the typically Victorian Valley Gardens, with bandstand: on gala nights there were candle-lamps for fairy-tale effect, there was an ornamental fountain, a chalybeate spring drinking fountain, croquet and bowls. At the glen's sheltered inner end is a more formal Italian Garden, and now also a miniature railway. In 1869 the valley was spanned by Halfpenny Bridge, of cross-girders supported on very slender iron columns, with delicate iron railings – the name came from the ½d. pedestrian toll, collected at a toll-booth at one end, and a toll-house, which survives, at the other. The bridge was demolished in 1974.

Saltburn, Cliff Lift. KIRKLEATHAM MUSEUM

Less of an aesthetic loss were the 1890 Brine Baths, in red brick with square tower, decorative terracotta on a Dutch gable masking the pitched roof. Sea water was pumped up and heated for swimming, the bath could be boarded over and used for bazaars and other winter functions: brine, much stronger than sea water, was brought in by rail, and stored in the tower for treatment baths. Demolished in 1976, the building stood opposite the railway station.

The station has a three-bay *porte-cochère*, its round arches separated by Tuscan pilasters carrying an entablature. The five-bay main elevation has matching arcading, the doorways with radial fanlights, tall windows with elaborate cast-iron frames, barley-sugar-twist columns dividing the paired lights. Inside on a platform wall is a tiled map of the North Eastern Railway. The station concourse has been converted to shops and the trains stop a short distance away at an apology for a station, apparently the progeny of a marriage between igloo and greenhouse, sharing a car park with a 'conservation' designed supermarket. This is ironic in a place which owes its existence to the railway, and promotes its Victorian image – even to the extent of providing old-fashioned galloping horses at its funfair.

93

Scarborough, N Yorkshire

14 miles (22.5 km) NW of Bridlington on A165

The Romans put a signal station (see 53, NY) on the headland here, Vikings settled around the Harbour and there was a medieval castle (53, NY), but there is also Regency Scarborough. Having enjoyed fame as a 17th-century spa, it became in the 18th century the first resort for sea-bathing.

Near the Castle the mainly Early English Church of St Mary was once of double-aisled cruciform plan, but lost its two west towers, north transept and chancel during the Civil War. The east window is now below the rebuilt central tower. On the south side are three rib-vaulted chapels with burial niches. Many

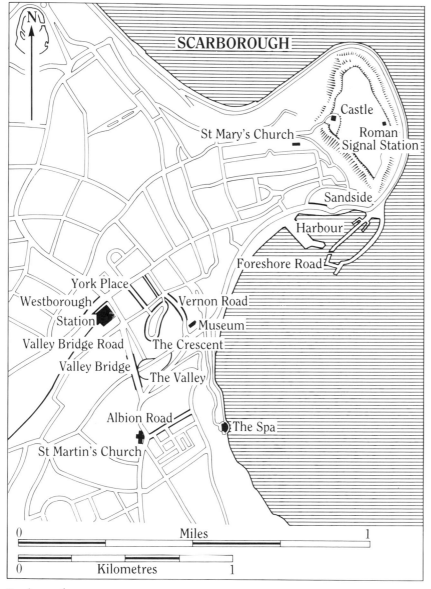

SCARBOROUGH

Scarborough. EH

entrance, vermiculated rusticated basement, red and orange terracotta, and window surrounds with Corinthian columns. Further south along the seafront is the Spa, with Baroque stonework, cast iron and glass, above the mineral spring discovered in the 17th century.

Funicular cliff lifts connect the beaches with the town far above, and the dramatically steep valley is spanned by cast-iron bridges. The pedestrian route up to the town passes the Museum, purpose-built to a design of 1828–9 by Richard Hey Sharp of York, with side wings added in 1860, and now housing archaeology and local history collections. The sandstone ashlar rotunda, with high-level small square windows between Tuscan pilasters, has a vertigo-inducing curving staircase, of even tighter curve to open upper level. Below the coffered dome curved mahogany cabinets used to display minerals and fossils – a travelling platform of 1838 allowed closer inspection! Male chauvinism relishes a ducking stool.

The Museum was part of a grandiose plan by Sharp and his younger brother Samuel for elegant terraces and villas. Several now house museum-related establishments: Wood End, the 1835 sandstone ashlar Regency villa later occupied by the Sitwell family, is now the Natural History Museum; Crescent House, enlarged in 1845 in a rather railway-like Italianate manner for solicitor John Uppleby, one of the Crescent developers, is now the Art Gallery; Londesborough Lodge, a c.1840 villa, now houses the Tourism and Amenities Department.

The Crescent, an impressive composition of two unequal curving sandstone ashlar terraces, is of three storeys plus basements, about an oval garden. Giant Tuscan pilasters delineate, paired doorways are architraved, windows are unsurrounded but have continuous cast-iron balconies to the first floor. The end houses are larger and project slightly, with Tuscan tripartite first-floor windows and bracketed doorcases.

Nearby in Vernon Road the Library, built in 1840 as the Oddfellows' Hall, is a

of the visitors come to see Anne Brontë's grave, by the north churchyard wall.

Alongside the Harbour, still a small working port, is a 'Dr Who'-type police box. There is 17th–18th-century brickwork, and snickets look as if they should contain some architectural treasures, but little that is medieval remains, except a fragment of timber-framing hiding at the side of the Newcastle Packet at the West Sandgate–

Sandside corner: King Richard III's house is partly Elizabethan.

From Foreshore Road is glimpsed Cuthbert Brodrick's 1863–7 Grand Hotel, from this distance a blur of a dozen or so floors of innumerable windows, cast-iron balconies, paired eaves brackets, and elaborate skyline, notably the coroneted corner domes with porthole windows. A climb to street level is rewarded by a shell-hooded classical composition with Ionic columns above shorter Tuscan columns. York Place is another elegant Regency terrace with full-height segmental bays: the similar Brunswick Terrace was replaced by a bland Brunswick Pavilion, where contrasting brickwork and blind arcading do little to mask lack of form.

From a roundabout at the junction of Westborough and Valley Bridge Road rises a vertical shaft over 20 ft (6 m) high, with blue neon lights, a period piece of Art Deco style. It superbly complements the adjacent 1936 Modernist building, formerly the Odeon Cinema, in brown brick and white terracotta, with ground-level black, and strips of red, an essay in vertical planes with a curved corner foyer in contrast, and carefully placed metal-framed windows.

G T Andrews' terminus railway station opened in 1845, with unusually long platforms for seasonal trains carrying large numbers of day-trippers, and there are canopies and slender suspension roofs, but the interior is plain by Andrews' standards. The Italianate ashlar sandstone exterior has three pedimented pavilions, and above the central one is a splendidly Baroque domed clock tower of 1882. Adjacent is the 1880s excursion station. Along

Westborough the monumental Methodist Church of 1862, in blackened ashlar sandstone, has a recessed portico with giant-order Corinthian columns, flanking turreted side bays, shell niches and bands of guilloche decoration.

In Albion Road among South Cliff genteel squares and terraces is the Church of St Martin-on-the-Hill, by George Frederick Bodley 1861. Plain, almost sombre externally, the interior is magnificently Pre-Raphaelite: fittings and decoration mainly designed by Bodley, executed by William Morris and firm – Ford Madox Brown, Dante Gabriel Rossetti, Edward Burne-Jones and Philip Webb. The east wall of the chancel, painted with red and green tracery, has panels of tile pictures – Adoration of the Magi, angels and saints. The triptych reredos has brattished canopy, to the north is a marble piscina, to the south a wooden sedile below tracery; there is a marble sanctuary floor, a chancel floor of alternate squares of marble and encaustic tiles and a painted chancel ceiling. To the north of the chancel is a delicate wrought-iron screen, to the south a large fretted woodwork organ case with a statue of St Martin. Below the tall chancel arch is a rood screen on marble shafts. The pulpit has painted panels, and everywhere is stained glass.

94
Whitby, N Yorkshire

19 miles (30 km) NW of Scarborough on A171

Whitby's picturesque quaysides line both sides of the River Esk's wide mouth, spanned by a swing bridge unless vessels are entering or leaving the harbour. On the west side G T Andrews' 1847 railway station brought some seaside visitors to George Hudson's West Cliff-top boarding house development, some of the terrace designs influenced by Newcastle-upon-Tyne architect John Dobson.

On the east side is the old centre, with quaint streets, and Market Place with 1788 classical Town Hall above open Tuscan ground-floor trading space. Buildings reflect the port's prosperity from the 17th-century export of alum from near Guisborough, the 18th-century whaling industry, and the carving of jet jewellery, made fashionable by Queen Victoria after Prince Albert's death.

Whitby Abbey (EH) is on the east cliff top. Here in AD 657 came Abbess Hilda from Hartlepool (see 37, C) to establish an abbey for both monks and nuns. One monk was Caedmon, herdsman turned poet, the first English hymn-writer. So great was this community's reputation, for justice as well as devotion, that in 664 the Northumbrian church's rival factions met here in synod to decide various disputed matters, including Easter dates. Among attenders was the young Wilfrid, later linked with Ripon Cathedral (33, NY).

The double monastery was abruptly destroyed by Danish invasion in 867, the site abandoned until in the 1070s Reinfrid, one of William the Conqueror's own knights, toured northern shrines. The site was then refounded as a Benedictine house, and an apsidal-ended cruciform church was constructed. So venerated was Hilda that this was soon too small to accommodate all the pilgrims, and in the 1220s Abbot Roger began a major, and over-ambitious, rebuilding.

The superb cliff-top setting gives

Scarborough Castle, town and harbour from the south-west. JB

additional prominence to the striking silhouette of the substantially complete Early English choir and north transept. Gables with tiered lancets are flanked by buttressed stair turrets crowned by conical turrets. The north aisle is still vaulted, a nave pier stands to full height, bearing a *graffito* date of 1790. Three nave arcade arches have been re-assembled against the south boundary wall, near the museum containing a replica Anglo-Saxon hand-loom, 1920s excavation having provided considerable evidence of the early nuns' spinning and weaving activities.

Post-Dissolution the site passed to the Cholmley family, who used much abbey stone to build Abbey House: the roofless shell of their Banqueting Hall, a 1670s severe classical building, stands to the south-west. By the car park is a tall monolithic medieval cross-shaft on a five-stepped circular base.

Also on the cliff top is the parish church of St Mary, essentially 12th-century in fabric but more famous for its little-altered Georgian interior. Mid-18th-century alterations included flat-headed small-paned nave windows, and round-headed south transept windows with keystones and intersecting glazing bars. A large north extension and Gothick south porch were added early in the 19th century. Also, the insertion of vast galleries necessitated the formation of verandah-like wooden external staircases for access.

The interior is a joy for those who can manage without an orderly west–east axis. Obscuring the Romanesque chancel arch the Cholmley Pew, its west face with cherubs and clock, stands on twisted Corinthian columns with volute capitals. In front is the three-decker pulpit of 1778, with serpent-like volutes above the tester, and huge ear trumpets for an early 19th-century rector's deaf wife. Box-pews are of various 17th- and 18th-century dates, those more important lined with green baize, others for free sittings. Marbled wooden Doric columns support white-fronted fielded panelled galleries and tall Gothick piers with acanthus capitals carry the north

Whitby Abbey from the churchyard. ES

extension, where Lord's Prayer and Commandments boards still have guidelines pencilled for the painter's lettering.

Ingeniously contrived clerestory windows, plus a splendid 1769 chandelier, help to illuminate the electric-light-free church. Below the tower are boards recording not only benefactions but also bell-ringing achievements, and a plank inscribed with the 1762 churchwardens' names. The large, windswept churchyard has a great variety of old tombstones, including many of master mariners. Those responsible for burying the dead in olden times faced the unenviable task of carrying them up the 'Church Stairs', the 199 steps which lead from Whitby old town.

95
York, N Yorkshire

24 miles (38.6 km) NE of Leeds on A64

No ancient city can offer standing evidence of more historic periods than York. This brief summary is chronological, not geographical. York has over 1900 years of recorded history, the Romans founding Eboracum (see 13, NY) in AD 71. The most important pre-Conquest ecclesiastical monument is the Anglo-Saxon tower of the church of St Mary, Bishophill Junior, which re-uses Roman stones, and an important Roman building, perhaps a Christian church, has been excavated beside it. The more famous Coppergate 'dig' has been turned into a much queued-for attraction, offering visitors not only the sights and sounds but also the smells of Viking Jorvik, from which York gets its modern name.

The Conquest gave York two Norman castles (see 45, NY). Many parish churches are partly Romanesque, including fine doorways at St Margaret, Walmgate and St Denys; of the many medieval churches, All Saints, North Street and Holy Trinity, Goodramgate are briefly mentioned under York Minster (see 44, NY), which encompasses all medieval periods. Near

its east end is St William's College, rebuilt in 1455–67 to house together its chantry priests, whose behaviour had attracted unfavourable comment; around a quadrangle, in York's magnesian limestone, its timber-framed upper floor is jettied out on carved brackets. Nearby in the Close the 17th- and 18th-century Treasurer's House [NT] was partly medievalised by Temple Moore c. 1900; next door in Gray's Court an original 12th-century wall stands to its second-floor corbel table, and there is a Jacobean long gallery.

Immediately outside the medieval city in its own walled precinct was the Benedictine St Mary's Abbey. Standing in its grounds the unusually early purpose-built Yorkshire Museum of 1827–30 is in scholarly Greek Revival by William Wilkins: its seemingly matching 1912 addition is not of stone but *in situ* concrete. York's many other medieval religious houses included St Leonard's very large hospital with up to 500 inmates, which extended from the vaulted undercroft near the Public Library to below the present Theatre Royal. A Georgian theatre rebuilt in 1877, Patrick Gwynne's 1967–8 addition of glazed reinforced-concrete hexagonal mushrooms is highly successful.

Tourists throng York's medieval streets, especially the famous Shambles, once the butchers' street, where upper storeys over-hang so much it is said neighbours opposite could shake hands, but there are many better and more authentic timber-framed buildings elsewhere, often hidden by later facades. The best timbered building open to the public is the Merchant Adventurers' Hall in Fossgate, its panelled two-aisled hall above an undercroft, which provided a hospital for aged brethren, the chapel with Puritan fittings.

That any timber-framed buildings, let alone so much beautiful medieval stained glass, have survived at all is miraculous, for Royalist York was besieged for several months in 1644 by Parliamentarians, so much late 17th-century reconstruction took place. The city's first nonconformist chapel, the Presbyterian, now Unitarian Church in St Saviourgate, a simple brick structure of Greek-cross plan with low central

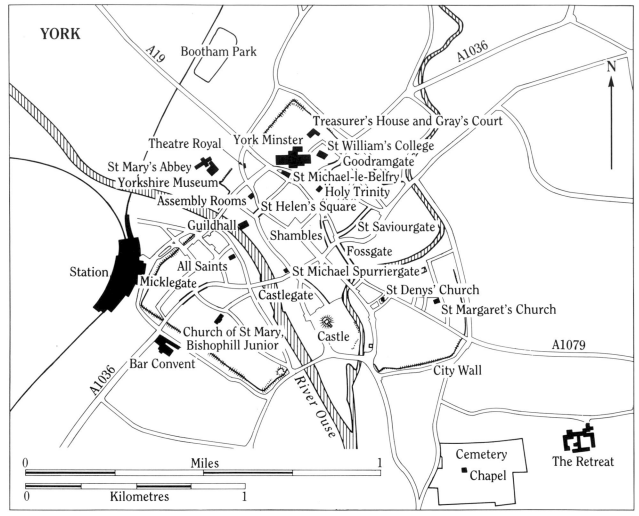

YORK

Bootham Park
A19
A1036
N

Theatre Royal
Treasurer's House and Gray's Court
York Minster
St William's College
St Mary's Abbey
Goodramgate
Yorkshire Museum
St Michael-le-Belfry
Assembly Rooms
Holy Trinity
St Helen's Square
Guildhall
St Saviourgate
Shambles
Fossgate
Station
St Michael Spurriergate
All Saints
St Denys' Church
Micklegate
Castlegate
St Margaret's Church
Church of St Mary,
Bishophill Junior
Castle
A1079
Bar Convent
River Ouse
City Wall
A1036

0   Miles   1
0   Kilometres   1

Cemetery
Chapel
The Retreat

York. EH

tower, was built in 1692–3.

Early 18th-century York, having lost trade as a river port, particularly for the staple cloth industry, was fortunate to become a social centre for the northern gentry's 'season'. The first of many fine public buildings was the elegant Mansion House of 1725–7 – probably designed by John Etty – in St Helen's Square. The city's coat of arms is in the pediment carried on giant-order Ionic pilasters, the first-floor two-storey state room, running the full five-bay width, is approached by a gracious staircase. The rusticated ground floor has round arches, one open to give access to the rear and to the Guildhall, reconstructed in 1958–61 after bomb damage. The history of York is told in the stained glass of its south window.

Gentry subscribed to build in 1730 the Assembly Rooms in Blake Street, designed by Lord Burlington and inspired by Palladio's Egyptian Hall. Its main hall, 40 yds (36 m) long, 40 ft (12 m) in height and width, has a pilastered clerestory with garlanded frieze carried on marbled Corinthian columns, arranged eighteen by six. Many activities enjoyed by the gentry centred on York Castle: county elections, and their heckling meetings, also courts and prisons – a hanging being a public spectacle. Castlegate was well placed for such recreation: Fairfax House, well restored and furnished by York Civic Trust, was fitted out by Viscount Fairfax of Gilling Castle (see 56, NY), who used only the best craftsmen, notably Giuseppe Cortese for exquisite plasterwork.

York has many fine Georgian town houses, several in Micklegate, some by John Carr, who lived nearby in Skeldergate. City streets were paved and lighted at night. The New Walk was created as a fashionable promenade by the River Ouse in the 1730s. A 1763 Act of Parliament forbade dripping eaves, so many houses were fitted with lead gutters and rain-water pipes in that year, the date on hopper-heads not necessarily dating construction.

Growing awareness of deprivation led to the establishment of charitable institutions such as almshouses, hospitals, schools. The County Lunatic Asylum (now Bootham Park), designed by John Carr in 1772–7, was considered so inhumane by Samuel Tuke that he founded The Retreat, the first of many endowments from members of the Society of Friends greatly to benefit York.

Several medieval churches were given good Georgian fittings, including sanctuary furniture in St Michael, Spurriergate, and St Michael-le-Belfry, High Petergate. A fine Roman Catholic chapel of 1766–9 by Thomas Atkinson graces the Bar Convent, just outside Micklegate Bar – now a Roman Catholic museum, it was a girls' school run by nuns of the Institute of the Blessed Virgin Mary, and founded by Mary Ward, a pioneer of girls' education, who died in York in 1645. The main Catholic church is George Goldie's St Wilfrid's of 1862–4, next to the Minster. The best surviving 19th-century nonconformist chapel is the Centenary Methodist Church in St Saviourgate, designed by James Simpson of Leeds in 1839–40. With its massive Ionic portico and elegant galleried interior, it was built to commemorate the centenary of Wesleyan Methodism.

In the 19th century York became a railway centre. The first station, designed by G T Andrews in 1840, was inside the city walls: gracious, with an attached hotel which survives as railway offices, it was soon too congested to function, as trains left the same way they had entered. The second station, designed by North Eastern Railway engineer Thomas Prosser in 1877, was built just outside the walls over an existing curving line, so the station had

York, Bootham Bar. From W Chambers Lefroy, *The Ruined Abbeys of Yorkshire*, 1883.

to do likewise, and the sweep of fanning cast-iron arched roof ribs is one of the spatial experiences of York. Visitors arriving by train when the daffodils are out on the city rampart opposite are met with a breath-taking sight.

To the visitor, York seems to have retained so much of its heritage. To this native it has lost in her lifetime much of value, but it is good to be able to end this entry on a happy note, the restoration of York Cemetery mortuary chapel of

1836–7 by the elder James Piggott Pritchett, after threat from decay. The Greek Ionic order, correctly used, creates a dignified and sober, but uplifting design: porticoed front, side columns *in antis*, all with pediments. The carefully planned cemetery has good ironwork by the distinguished Walker foundry of York. The monuments not only provide invaluable historical information, but are a catalogue of changing tastes in the 19th century.

8

Industry, Communications and Municipal Buildings

The process often called the Industrial Revolution, a phenomenon with which the region is much associated, occurred here for reasons of physical geography: the availability of raw materials such as coal and iron, and wool from sheep; and heavy Pennine rainfall swelled swift-flowing streams which fell steeply from high to low levels, giving sites good for water power. Another important factor was the unusually high number – as reflected in the size of chapter 2 – of monastic houses. These, particularly of the Cistercian order, instigated growth in the cloth industry, encouraged developments in corn-grinding machinery, improved techniques for metal smelting and brewing, and above all improved road communications.

The first chore to be mechanised was corn grinding, using water power. The Domesday Book shows that corn watermills were relatively commonplace by 1086: one such mill then in existence was at **Crakehall** (100, NY). About a thousand years after the Romans introduced water power, the wind was harnessed for corn grinding, a development which first took place in the twelfth century in East Riding, the area in which **Skidby Windmill** (107, H) is located.

The next task mechanised was the fulling of medieval cloth by water, but it took many centuries for the many other textile processes to be powered. Halifax (84, WY), the leading cloth centre of the water-powered era, is a settlement in chapter 7, its Piece Hall a monument of great national significance. Bradford (81, WY) is of similar importance in the history of steam-powered textile production. **Saltaire** (106, WY) is remarkable as an industrial settlement, with its huge textile mill and complete model village.

Communications history begins in this book with the Wheeldale Moor Roman Road (12, NY), and continues in this chapter with two of the country's four medieval bridges still with chantry chapels, at **Rotherham** (97, SY) and **Wakefield** (98, WY), the other two being at Bradford-on-Avon and St Ives. The region contains many fine 18th-century bridges designed by John Carr (who served as bridge-master to both North and West Ridings) such as that at Richmond (90, NY), mentioned briefly in chapter 7. Two of the individual entries in this chapter are bridges included for technological interest, **Middlesbrough Transporter Bridge** (103, C) and the **Humber Bridge** (102, H).

Canal structures are represented by the splendid Five Rise Locks at **Bingley** (101, WY) and the Leeds and Liverpool Canal warehouse in Leeds (88, WY). Railway stations mentioned in chapter 7 are York's two stations (95, NY), the 'Jacobethan' example at Richmond (90, NY), and those at Hull (87, H) and Saltburn (92, C) which had attached hotels. Also worthy of a visit is the splendid railway station at Huddersfield (excluded here due to constraints of space), which has end pavilions flanking a Corinthian portico, housing the all-important clock. The seaport of Hull (87, H) merits an entry in chapter 7, as does the river port of Goole (83, H), a remarkable example of industrial heritage. On the coast is the early lighthouse at **Flamborough** (104, H).

Public buildings fall into a number of categories, and many are included in chapter 7. Some had a commercial role, such as the elegant Market Cross at **Pontefract** (105, WY), or the impressive Corn Exchange in Leeds (see 88, WY). There are fine Victorian indoor market halls in Halifax (84, WY) and Leeds. In the 18th century many settlements erected fine buildings for public functions, such as York's Mansion House and Assembly Rooms (95, NY). Doncaster also has an important Mansion House, designed by James Paine in 1745. The town halls at Richmond (90, NY), and Ripon (see 33, NY) were also built for public

Humber Bridge. DIS

Huddersfield railway station in 1972. JH

explanation of the purpose of this group of buildings, founded as a hospital, or almshouse, in 1593 by Lady Margaret Russell, wife of George Clifford, 3rd earl of Cumberland.

Their remarkable daughter Lady Anne Clifford, when dowager countess of Pembroke, Dorset and Montgomery, added to it in 1650–60 (see 59, NY). Lady Anne frequently occurs in northern history, a formidable lady who made journeys, daunting to lesser mortals, through wild terrain between her various properties. She added the roadside block of cottages, which have double-chamfered mullion windows, and door surrounds of various designs.

The eye travels over sensitive floorscaping, of York stone paving and setts, up a rising straight path slightly off-line from the carriageway, to Lady Margaret's remarkable hospital. Of two concentric stone circles, it has a central plan about a vertical axis: the inner wall rises up above the main steeply sloping stone slate roof to form the drum of a domed roof; in the drum are mullion windows, and large chimney-stacks rise from it.

At the top of the path a Tudor-arched doorway gives onto a stone-flagged

functions, but the term Town Hall now reflects the bureaucratic use to which these buildings were later put.

Changes and increases in municipal administration in Victorian times resulted in the construction of purpose-built town halls, of which that at Leeds (see 88, WY) is an extremely grand example. By the late 19th century new units of administration necessitated buildings such as **County Hall, North-allerton** (99, NY).

Some buildings catered for public entertainment, such as Richmond's grandstand and theatre (see 90, NY), or of more modern date Scarborough's Odeon Cinema (see 93, NY). Private benefaction resulted in the unusual **Beamsley Hospital** (96, NY), a rare example of a practical building which resembles a folly. Other almshouses included elsewhere in the volume are at Coxwold (82, NY) and Kirkleatham (34, C).

96
Beamsley Hospital, N Yorkshire
16th–17th century

SE 077529. 6 miles (9.6 km) E of Skipton and just to N of Beamsley, beside A59 Skipton–Harrogate road

[B] LT Viewing by appointment with housekeeper, tel. Skipton 795461

A high stone wall beside a section of the old road now shields from the busy A59's roar a haven of peace and piety dating back to the reign of the first Queen Elizabeth. Through a Tudor-arched opening can be glimpsed two similar arches, forming a carriageway which passes centrally through a building. Above the first arch a panel bears two coats of arms; within the carriageway a lengthy inscription gives some

Beamsley Hospital. LT

passage, leading to the central space. This is the chapel, top-lit from the dome, still as furnished by Lady Anne. There is no eastward orientation, for this was the Puritan period, when preaching was far more important than the sacraments, and so there is a large pulpit, and small pews.

Opposite the entrance is a single triangular-headed door, and on either side are paired simpler doors: the single one led to the room of the Mother of the community, the others to those of four of her Sisters, a further two Sisters having doors off the entrance passage. Each of these six curving rooms had a Tudor-arched fireplace. A further six inmates lived in the entrance range. This arrangement survived little changed until the 1970s, since when the outer range remains an almshouse, but the circular block is a carefully adapted holiday cottage which retains the chapel unaltered.

97
Bridge and Chantry Chapel of All Saints, Rotherham, S Yorkshire
15th century

SK 429936. NW of Rotherham centre

[C]

The bridge at All Saints, with its four arches of unchamfered ribs, is a rare survival. Medieval bridges over major rivers were few and far between, because of the technical difficulties of erecting a structure which had to rest on the river bed. Travelling in medieval times was extremely hazardous, and it was customary to call into a church or chapel to pray, both before setting out, and after a safe return. Chapels were often therefore provided on or near medieval bridges, sometimes by a benefactor who was contributing also to the bridge. Endowing such a chapel as a chantry, where mass would be celebrated daily for the soul of the founder, provided a priest for the benefit of travellers, and was likely also to ensure additional prayer for the

Rotherham, bridge and chantry chapel of All Saints. ROTHERHAM CENTRAL LIBRARY

founder's soul from the grateful laity.

On a large island between the main River Don and a flood channel is All Saints' chantry chapel, built in 1483 and now used for a weekly service of Holy Communion. A small two-bay cell in red ashlar sandstone, it has crenellated parapets and pinnacles. The west doorway from the bridge roadway has a continuously moulded Tudor arch and hood-mould. The windows, of three lights to the north and south, two to the west and four lights to the east, have Perpendicular tracery. Below is a tunnel-vaulted crypt with small chamfered light vents with iron stanchions.

98
Bridge and Chantry Chapel of St Mary, Wakefield, W Yorkshire
14th and 19th century

SE 336201. Alongside A61 Barnsley road, just S of Wakefield city centre

[D]

The medieval bridge over the River Calder has nine pointed arches with chamfered ribs. On an island on the east side is the small chapel, licensed as a

Wakefield, bridge and chantry chapel of St Mary. WAKEFIELD MDC

chantry in 1357. Considered the finest surviving bridge chapel in the country, it was restored by Sir George Gilbert Scott in 1847, having long been neglected.

The chapel is an unusually florid example of the fully Decorated Gothic style, the five-light east window has a four-centred arch and curvilinear tracery, the three straight-headed north and south windows have three lights. The parapet is arcaded, and at the north-east corner an octagonal turret sits above a spiral staircase descending to a sacristy below.

The entrance elevation from the bridge roadway is a replacement by Scott, with five arches below crocketed gablets, three forming doorways, below a sculptured pierced parapet with corner pinnacles. The original west facade was re-erected as a boat-house 2 miles (3.2 km) away beside the lake at Kettlethorpe Hall, a fine house of 1727 restored in 1990 by the Yorkshire Buildings Preservation Trust.

99
County Hall, Northallerton, N Yorkshire
20th century

SE 365932. Just S of Northallerton town centre, on E side of A167

[D]

Walter Brierley succeeded to the York architectural practice that John Carr had founded, and also acted as North Riding county architect in 1901–22, hence his many fine school buildings. He is particularly known for the country houses he built, extended or altered, with a sensitive eye for period detail and quality craftsmanship, such as Sledmere House (77, H).

County Hall of 1904–6 was his largest single design commission, added to many times since. Its setting is typical of Brierley, gracious lawns with formal ponds and colourful flower-beds, and softer planting of shrubs of many sizes, shapes, textures and colours around the edges. The iron gates and perimeter railings are elegant but not ostentatious.

Brierley gave County Hall a Baroque-style grandeur, externally Wren-like, skilfully massed in brick with ashlar dressings, with neo-Georgian interiors. The U-shaped plan consists of an imposing main block containing meeting rooms on the first floor and running off behind each end a two-storey office wing with long spine corridors. Sash windows have stone architraves, segmental-arched and keyed to the ground floor. The central entrance is emphasised with greater height and increased use of stone, and a giant Corinthian order carries a central

pedimented feature and attic storey.

The Vanbrugh-like interior has interesting spatial relationships and fine finishes. The splendid entrance hall leads to the imposing imperial-plan main staircase, with much marble and grandeur, the council chamber at half-landing level. A groin-vaulted first-floor corridor, with windows on inner side, runs the length of the front block. In the centre is the Grand Committee Room, its walls with giant-order Corinthian columns carrying an overhanging cornice below a coved ceiling; the doors with segmental pediments, the fireplace

County Hall, Northallerton, Grand Committee Room. HMK

112

a pedimented over-mantel; the furniture is long curving tables.

The lesser committee rooms have a graduated progression of decreasingly elaborate details, some rooms Ionic, some Doric. All have a fireplace as an axial feature, and decorative plasterwork on segmentally vaulted ceilings. The doors, in elegant cases, are of very high-quality hardwood. Minor details, such as door furniture and light fittings, are excellent examples of Arts and Crafts Movement design.

100

Crakehall Watermill, N Yorkshire
17th-19th century

SE 242902. N of A684 in Crakehall, 9 miles (14.4 km) SW of Northallerton

[A]

Crakehall Watermill. Drawing by J E Daughters. P H TOWNSEND

There was a corn watermill here at the time of the Domesday Survey of 1086. For much of the medieval period it belonged to the Neville family of Middleham, but their property later passed to the Crown, and when James I sold the manor of Crakehall in 1624, the mill fell into private hands.

At least some of its stonework dates from rebuilding and enlargement *c*.1625. Close examination of the mill fabric by the author in 1976 showed that the wheelhouse was designed for two small undershot waterwheels, each driving one pair of millstones inside the mill. A single larger breastshot waterwheel was installed early in the 19th century to drive four pairs of millstones, the spur gearing which made this possible being adopted late by northern country corn millers.

The frame of the present cast-iron waterwheel was made by F Mattison and Company, the local iron foundry at Leeming Bar near Bedale, in 1898. The wooden furniture around the millstones faithfully replicates that in place when the mill closed in the 1920s. Typical of rural corn mills, it was renewed in 1980 when the mill was restored for use once more.

In the 17th and 18th centuries the mill needed only two storeys, a ground floor for gearing, and a first for millstones. During the early 19th century the function of the country miller changed: instead of grinding small quantities of corn which people had grown for themselves, and keeping a proportion of it as a toll, he became a dealer in corn and flour for people who did not grow their own. This required dry storage and so many country mills, like Crakehall, had a top storey added.

The large pond which stores water taken from Bedale Beck, by means of a weir near Crakehall Bridge, had completely silted up during the period of inactivity, and had to be re-excavated before the wheel could turn again.

101

Five Rise Locks, Bingley, W Yorkshire
18th century

SE 108399. 1 mile (1.6 km) SE of Bingley railway station and N of A650(T)

[D]

The Leeds and Liverpool Canal was a man-made canal (as opposed to a river made navigable) created under a 1770 Act of Parliament. Climbing steeply up towards the watershed of the Pennines, here near Bingley the canal ascends by a staggering staircase of five locks, high above the town. The canal is the only trans-Pennine waterway route not to have closed, although now it is used mainly for recreational rather than commercial purposes.

The locks, constructed in ashlar millstone grit, have a rugged quality – well maintained, even a little cherished, they are functional. There is only one touch of sentiment, the informative plaque put up on the bicentenary of their construction, which reads:

The Five-Rise Locks Designed By John Longbotham of Halifax And Built in 1774 By Local Stonemasons Barnabus Morvil, Jonathan Farrar, William Wild all of Bingley and John Sugden from Wilsden. The Locks Raise Boats 59ft. 2ins. Over A Distance Of 320ft. Distance By Canal To Leeds 16 miles 2 furlongs To Liverpool 111 miles.

Five Rise Locks, Bingley, *c*.1920. BRITISH WATERWAYS

There is a lock-keeper's house, and office, and a swing footbridge. Boats queuing to use the locks can wait in a pound. It is brilliant, but understated: this is the stuff of which the Industrial Revolution was made in Yorkshire.

102

Humber Bridge, Humberside
20th century

TA 0223. Carries A15 across Humber estuary, linking Hessle with Barton-upon-Humber

[C]

The world's longest single-span suspension bridge, with an overall length of 2,428 yds (2,220 m), was opened by HM the Queen on 17 July 1981. The extremely beautiful structure is so large that cars and lorries seem as toys, just glinting in the sun. The two pylons, 510 ft (155 m) high, were, for the first time in a major suspension bridge, built of reinforced concrete, not steel. It was designed by Bernard Wex, the consulting engineers being Freeman, Fox and Partners.

The bridge deck hangs from the suspension cables by such delicate ropes that they give no sense of security to drivers high above and far out into the estuary, but form a design of V-shapes. The structure is so important a landmark that viewpoints are provided. It looks particularly impressive at night, with red lights on pylons and paired yellow lights of lamp-standards on the central reservation picking out the bridge deck's subtle convex arch.

103

Middlesbrough Transporter Bridge, Cleveland
20th century

NZ 500213. Middlesbrough, E of Stockton-on-Tees. Ferry Road, in town centre

[D]

A prominent feature of the industrial skyline of the low-lying Teesside connurbation, the bridge replaced a ferry between Middlesbrough and Billingham. Consultation in 1906 with F Arnondi, pioneer of this kind of structure, preceded the decision to proceed with the design, and the promotional bill received royal assent in 1907. The bridge was opened by HRH

Prince Arthur, Duke of Connaught on 17 October 1911. Its advantage is that no bridge deck obstructs the shipping routes on the river below.

Of sixteen transporter bridges constructed throughout the world, only six survive. Built of steel, to which two coats of red lead priming paint were originally applied, it is now painted blue. The contractor was William Arrol and Company. There are four pylons, in two pairs, standing about 202 yds (185 m) apart, from which are cantilevered two asymmetrical triangular trusses. The bottom chords of these are linked to support the travelling frame.

Suspended from the frame by sixty wire ropes is the travelling car, moved by an endless rope system worked from an electrically driven winch on the Middlesbrough bank, the journey across the river taking a little over two minutes. The car, approximately 13 yds (12 m) by 15 yds (14 m), was designed to hold 860 passengers, is now restricted to 600, and to 9 cars, but can transport about 1,000 vehicles and 1,100 foot passengers per day.

The original charge for pedestrians was 1d., but they were charged 3d. for climbing the 209 steps to the gangway at the height of the travelling frame, over 165 ft (50 m) above high-water level. This walkway has been closed since 1981 because of suicide attempts.

104
Old Lighthouse, Flamborough, Humberside
17th century

TA 247707. Near end of B1259 road at Flamborough Head, 5 miles (8 km) NE of Bridlington

[D]

Now surrounded by a golf course, this lighthouse was erected in 1674 by Sir John Clayton to guide mariners passing near the treacherous rocky coast. Octagonal in plan, built in coursed, but now weathered, chalk rubble, and four stages high, the stages are marked by sandstone bands of bird's beak section.

The purpose of the tower was to elevate the beacon and to provide access to the top, surrounded by a brick parapet, where it was lit. Openings are restricted to the sides facing the cardinal points: the west side only has a pointed-arched ground-floor doorway, the south side a slightly more elaborate entrance with Gothick brickwork, and the north side a small ground-floor window. On the three upper stages to north, east and south are chamfered single-light windows, their sandstone surrounds standing proud of the chalk walls.

The Old Lighthouse, though still used by local fishermen as a visual

Flamborough, Old Lighthouse. JH

navigational aid, was superseded by John Matson's present lighthouse in 1806. The latter is to be automated in 1995, and until then will be the last manned lighthouse on the east coast.

In Flamborough village the Church of St Oswald contains Bridlington Priory's rood screen with loft, and another fine medieval screen between chancel and chapel, both the work of the famous Bromflet family of Ripon woodcarvers. The church contains the chest tomb to Sir Marmaduke Constable, died 1520, with lengthy brass inscription in black letter style, giving his biography as a knight whose career stretched from Edward IV's to Henry VII's campaigns.

Middlesbrough Transporter Bridge. CCL

115

Pontefract market cross in 1942. RCHME

105
Pontefract Market Cross, W Yorkshire
18th century

SE 455218. Market Place, Pontefract
[D]

Pontefract retains several good Georgian buildings, including a hotel, former town hall, bank, parish church, town houses and this excellent market building on the site of a medieval cross. It was built in 1734 by Elizabeth Dupier in memory of her husband Solomon, one of the garrison at Gibraltar when it was besieged by Spaniards in 1727.

Such buildings had many functions; they added dignity to a civic space when people were becoming more aware of the importance of elegant buildings; they provided some shelter from the elements, keeping vendors dry, but also giving some shade for perishable goods such as butter; and their raised level floor was a distinct advantage when market places were regularly traversed by horses, cattle, sheep, etc.

Pontefract's market cross is set on a podium of rectangular plan with arched openings, one at each end, three to the sides. The ashlar stonework is rusticated up to the imposts of the round arches with keyed archivolts. A cornice articulates the local stone slate hipped roof, which in 1763 replaced a balustraded flat roof. Inside is a long plank bench, and on the outside a mid-18th-century water pump has raised foliage decoration on its lead casing.

106
Saltaire Mill and Model Village, W Yorkshire
19th century

SE 140381. N of A650 Shipley–Keighley road, ¾ mile (1.2 km) NW of Shipley
[C]

Sir Titus Salt had made a fortune from importing the wool of the alpaca, a llama-like animal from Peru, when he decided late in 1850 to build a huge new mill and model village, on the south bank of the River Aire – necessary for the textile processes – hence the name. Europe's largest textile mill opened in 1853 to tremendous celebration, the structure designed by engineer Sir William Fairbairn, the Italianate

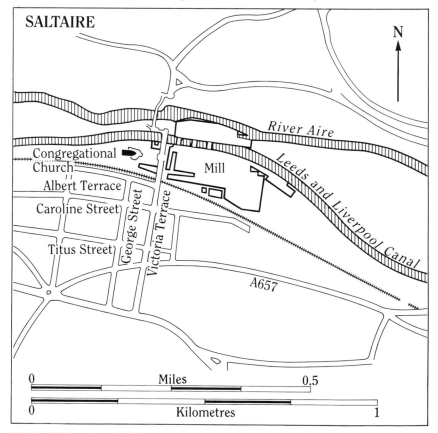

Saltaire Mill and model village. EH

exteriors by architects Lockwood and Mawson. Very carefully situated, a campanile-like chimney faces the Leeds and Liverpool Canal, an obelisk-like chimney fronts the railway line.

Almost as presentable internally as externally, the cast-iron columns having acanthus capitals, it has since closure in 1986 been converted to accommodate several new uses, including an art gallery. The resurgence has caught on: the reopened railway station serves commuters as well as visitors, and a water-bus operates on the canal. The valley also remains the scenic attraction it was when Salt chose the site.

The sandstone grid-plan model village is also by Lockwood and Mawson, the leading Bradford architects of their day. The sloping streets were named after the children of Salt, the royal family, and the designers – Caroline, George, Ada, Edward, Fanny, Mary, Helen, Henrietta, etc. The houses, mildly classical in style, are of several sizes, not to accommodate differing family units, but to reflect the relative status of the mill's employees. All temperate facilities were provided: hospital, almshouse, school, institute-cum-library, park and a Congregational Church which could not possibly be called a chapel.

The church, itself of conventional rectangular plan, has a front portico of Corinthian columns, curving spectacularly to enclose the rounded base of the superbly ornate cupola. At the side is the apsidal-ended Salt Mausoleum, with sunbursts in round arches below a lead dome.

Skidby Windmill. DIS

107
Skidby Windmill, Humberside
19th century

TA 020333. ¼ mile (0.4 km) S of Skidby, alongside A164 Beverley–Hessle road

[A]

The first recorded English windmill was in 1185 at Weedley in the old East Riding of Yorkshire. Areas like the Pennine Dales had excellent steeply falling streams for driving waterwheels, but flat plains and plateaux tops had to rely on wind for power until the advent of steam power. Humberside is therefore an area with a windmill heritage, but few are complete.

Skidby Windmill, built in 1821, has a tall seven-storey brick tower, and Lincolnshire-type ogee dome, complete with four sails and fantail. From the middle level projects a balcony, from which the ends of the sails can be reached for adjustment. Corn-grinding machinery in windmills was over-driven, whereas watermills are usually under-driven.

The date is reflected in the large structure at Skidby – earlier windmills being much smaller in scale, and with smaller sails – and it forms a prominent landmark sited on a low hill in gentle Wolds countryside.

Select Bibliography

Many of the properties in this volume, particularly those in National Trust or English Heritage guardianship, have their own guide publications, and there are many well-known standard works on the general categories of buildings here included. The following list may be regarded as supplementary to those.

Geoffrey Beard, *Decorative Plasterwork in Great Britain*, Phaidon, 1975.

British Archaeological Association, *The East Riding of Yorkshire*, BAA Conference Transactions, 1989.

Howard Colvin, *A Biographical Dictionary of British Architects 1600–1840*, John Murray, 1978.

Mark Girouard, *The English Town*, Yale University Press, 1990.

Jane Hatcher, *The Industrial Architecture of Yorkshire*, Phillimore, 1985.

Jane Hatcher, *Richmondshire Architecture* (privately published), 1990.

Christopher Hussey, *English Country Houses* (3 vols.), *Country Life*, 1958.

John Hutchinson and D M Palliser, *York*, John Bartholomew, 1980.

James Lang, *Anglo-Saxon Sculpture*, Shire Publications, 1988.

Derek Linstrum, *West Yorkshire Architects and Architecture*, Lund Humphries, 1978.

Patrick Nuttgens, *Brierley in Yorkshire*, York Georgian Society, 1984.

Colin Platt, *Abbeys of Yorkshire*, English Heritage, 1988.

D N Riley, *Yorkshire's Past from the Air*, Sheffield Academic Press, 1988.

Royal Commission on the Historical Monuments of England, *Beverley: An Archaeological and Architectural Study*, HMSO, 1982.

Royal Commission on the Historical Monuments of England, *The City of York* (5 vols), HMSO, 1962–81.

York Georgian Society, *The Works in Architecture of John Carr*, YGS, 1973.

Index

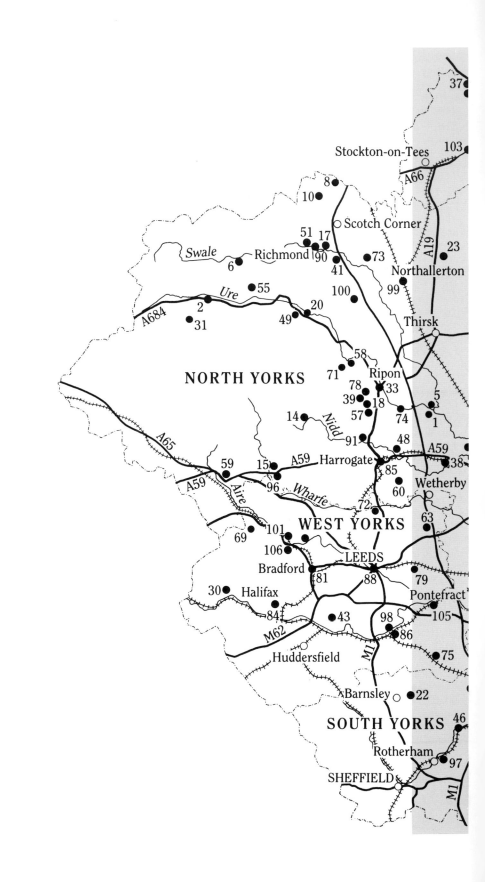

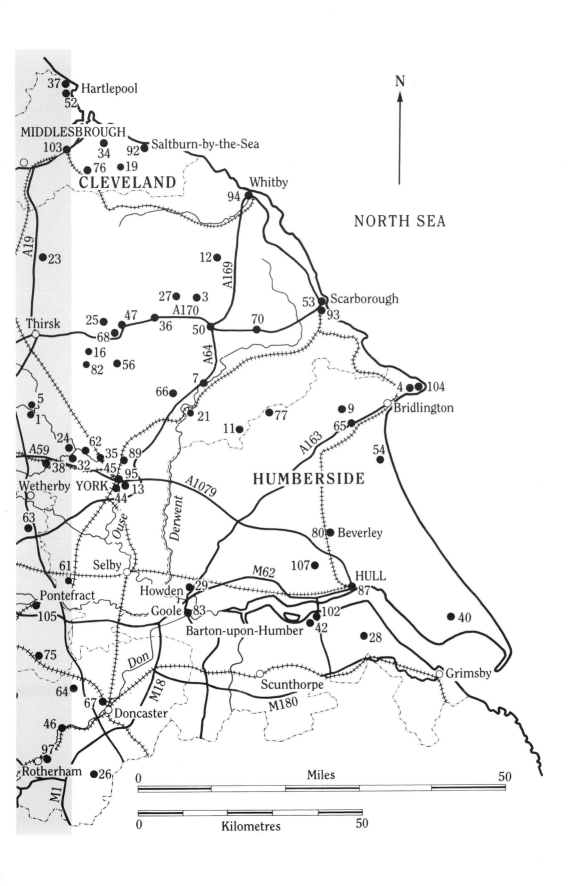

N

37 Hartlepool
52
MIDDLESBROUGH
103
34 92 Saltburn-by-the-Sea
76 19
CLEVELAND
94 Whitby

NORTH SEA

23

12
A169

27 3
53 Scarborough
25 47 A170 70 93
68 36 50
Thirsk
16
82 56
A64
7
66 4 104
21 Bridlington
11 77 9
A163 65
54
5
1
24 62
A59 35 89 HUMBERSIDE
38 32 45
95
Wetherby YORK 13
44
Ouse Derwent A1079
63
80 Beverley
61 Selby
M62 107
Pontefract Howden 29 HULL
105 Goole 83 87
Barton-upon-Humber 102
42 40
28
75 Don
64 M18 Scunthorpe Grimsby
67 M180
46 Doncaster
97
Rotherham 26
M1

0 Miles 50

0 Kilometres 50